A GREAT AND HUMBLE SOUL

Marie Victoire Couderc
MOTHER THÉRÈSE

Henry Perroy, S.J.

A Great and
Humble Soul

MOTHER THÉRÈSE COUDERC

Foundress of the Congregation of Our Lady of the Retreat
in the Cenacle

(1805-1885)

Translated from the French by
JOHN J. BURKE, C.S.P., S.T.D.

1960
THE NEWMAN PRESS
WESTMINSTER, MARYLAND

First published 1933
Reprinted 1960

Nihil obstat: JOHN G. HOGAN
Diocesan Censor

Imprimatur: ✠ RICHARD CARDINAL CUSHING
Archbishop of Boston

May 19, 1960

The *nihil obstat* and *imprimatur* are official declarations that a book or pamphlet is free of doctrinal and moral error. No implication is contained therein that those who have granted the *nihil obstat* and *imprimatur* agree with the opinions expressed.

In regard to the name "saint" or similar expressions in this book, the author declares that he intends nothing more than is implied in the commonly accepted sense of the words and does not in any way anticipate the infallible judgment of Holy Mother Church.

Contents

Translator's Foreword

SILENCE IS a virtue little known to our talkative and noisy world. To bring home to us its worth, Our Blessed Lord chooses now and then those among His devoted children who will, in a special way, illustrate and emphasize it in their own lives.

This present biography opens in a simple, commonplace manner. The first chapters may seem to promise nothing of interesting achievement. Let the reader read on, and he will see that out of the small efforts, the mistakes and the misunderstandings unfolds a story amazing and all but incredible.

Deposed as superior, deprived of the title of Foundress of the community she had established, the heroine of this story lived, save for two notable events, in silence for decades, so that she became almost unknown, and was all but unnoticed, in her own community. Shortly before the end, her glory is revealed: but the mystery of her silence remains to reprove and to inspire.

Out of her silence has grown the extensive retreat work of the Religious of the Cenacle. That work has led unnumbered thousands to enter into

silence and learn therein of the life of Our Blessed
Lord in their souls and of their life in Him. The
Mother's silence is still the interior, abiding secret
of every daughter of the Cenacle. Their labors also
make it eloquent throughout the whole world.

The life told of in this volume recalls those
words of a Catholic poet on the silence of Our
Blessed Lady:

"Thou Speaker of all wisdom in a Word,
    Thy Lord.
Speaker who thus could well afford
Thence to be silent; ah, what silence that
Which had for prologue thy 'Magnificat'?
O, Silence full of wonders,
More than by Moses in the Mount were heard,
More than were uttered by the Seven Thunders;
Silence, that crowns, unnoted, like the voiceless
    blue,
The loud world's varying view,
And in its holy heart the sense of all things
    ponders!"

Feast of the Holy Name of Mary,
*   September 12, 1933.*

PART ONE

The Dawn

I. Le Mas

MARIE VICTOIRE COUDERC was born on the first day of February, 1805, in one of the hamlets of Sablières, a village of the department of Ardèche.

Her family was not of the nobility, neither was it entirely of the peasant class. It had secured in the community its own worthy position such as, unfortunately, is unknown to families whose too rapid advancement impedes further progress.

Le Mas was a large farm almost four miles in length. There the Couderc family led a quiet but laborious life. Their land was their treasure.

The little Marie Victoire and her sister Ursula were but two of a large number of children born between 1802 and 1825.

It is often well that a young girl have many brothers. From daily companionship with them her characteristics will take on something of the manly and the vigorous. The father and mother of this large family, moreover, gave them rigid training. A sort of monitor of penitents, father Couderc would resent it if during the evening prayers anyone spoke. The parish curé of Sablières termed mother Couderc "the strong woman." He would say with pleasantry, "In Sablières and its fourteen hamlets, there are in all but three women. Of these, I would give first place to Madame Couderc." One fact—to cite only one—which confirmed the curé's judgment is the following, which many Christians, living in large cities with many churches, might well ponder.

Le Mas was almost three miles from Sablières—a full hour's journey. There was no road, only paths used by mule drivers. In winter these tracks were covered with snow. Yet twice a week, Mondays and Fridays, Madame Couderc went to Sablières to assist at Holy Mass. On those days she rose at four o'clock. Happy the pastors who count among their flock souls of such vigor! Happy the children who have such a mother!

The sure result followed. God came knocking upon their door, certain of His answer.

The two eldest, John and Marie Victoire, first heard the divine call.

The call invitingly revealed itself to the boy through his desire to offer Mass: to the girl, through her longing to serve Mass. The altar was poor enough. Marie Victoire, in lieu of a vestment, would put her blue or white apron on her brother's shoulders. Oftentimes at evening around the large family table, or beside the chimney, crackling with pine branches, the parents would recount to the children how during the days of the Terror, priests offered Mass in the attic. Their own father had kept watch at the windows. More than once the ceremony had been suddenly interrupted, and the priest had to seek a secret hiding place in the wall. Never did the young sentinel fail in his watchfulness. Sometimes these priests of God would be compelled to hide for days within the caves on the Couderc property, but not one was ever captured by the authorities. Twenty small eyes followed that dramatic story told by father and again by mother.

Marie Victoire, already practical in her piety, would the next day visit the places made holy by the presence of these priests of God. Alone, or with John, her little priest of the morning, she would go to the grottoes, to the attic, wherever they told her these priests had hidden.

These first impressions influenced her soul. This vision of persecuted priests taught her sacrifice. Her sister, Ursula, who shared her bedroom, told later how at night, Marie Victoire kneeling upon the bed, with hands joined, would beg God to make her a religious.

The infant prayer winged its way to God. It was not the first time God had heard with favor the prayer of little hands in suppliant gesture, speaking the ardent desire of the heart to be wholly His.

* * *

But the religious life is as yet far away. Just now the little one must learn to read and write.

At that time there were no school teachers in

the villages. France was still seeking to raise battalions rather than to establish schools. At Sablières, an elderly woman, Catherine Boyer, through her zeal, gathered together some children of the neighboring hamlets. A sort of eccentric saint, this Catherine Boyer, her hair arranged in the customary way but crowned by a hat of long, long ago.

To her, for lack of a better teacher, the Coudercs entrusted Marie Victoire. But Catherine did not succeed in teaching Marie how to spell. During these years, Marie spelled as she spoke, unembarrassed by the subtleties of grammar. But if she did not learn how to spell, she did learn her catechism. When the curé of Sablières passed her for First Holy Communion, he said: "I have never seen a child better prepared than Marie Victoire to receive our Saviour, Jesus Christ."

The divine meeting took place on the day of Pentecost, 1815. It was a great feast day at Le Mas. John, three years older than his sister, had the same blessed happiness as she. Not without a purpose did God unite these two children of His choice in the presence of the Blessed Sacrament. One was to be a priest; the other, the foundress of a religious order.

After devout pilgrimages to the grottoes made holy by the persecuted priests, after the childlike Masses said together, these two are now on their knees before the one ciborium. The reception of the Holy Eucharist threw over their intimacy a seriousness, I know not of what gravity, which ever afterwards endured. From the hour that John left for the seminary, Marie Victoire ceased to speak to him in the old familiar way. But the rays from the ostensorium won their unfolding souls as rays of the sun the morning rose. What Madame Couderc did twice a week, Marie Victoire obtained permission to do once a week, summer and winter. Departing for Mass before four o'clock, she did not return till the sounding of the mid-day Angelus. "I love to be alone in prayer," she would say. These mornings of prayer, for she was left without other duty than some small errands from her mother, were her happiest.

The Holy Spirit gave then to His elect that which was to characterize her even to the end of her life: the gift of prayer. Was not the tribune at Fourvière a witness through the years of her long prayers? Solitary prayers in the church at Sablières, solitary prayers in the chapel of the Cenacle—and between the two—one of the most beautiful of the works that have come forth from the Heart of God!

The action of God bespeaks a marvelous unity. The prayer of the little child was the prelude to the work of the morrow. The prayer of the grown religious completed the prayer of hopeful vigil. Already the whole of the Cenacle, like unto that of Jerusalem, may be summed up by the words "in prayer." [1]

* * *

A Great and Humble Soul

One day, the fruit so slowly forming on this mysterious branch, ripened by the sun of the Tabernacle, quietly fell to earth. "I would like to be a religious," Marie Victoire told her parents. But the young child with the little white bonnet had not anticipated her father's answer. "How can you think of leaving Le Mas? Your mother's health is delicate. Ursula is still too young to be of help. It is necessary that you stay here."

She did stay. But a short time afterwards, sitting with her sister in a grassy field, Marie Victoire suddenly began to cry. "What is the matter with you?" asked her younger sister. "It's because they don't want me to become a religious." Nothing more surely touches the Heart of God than the tears of desire. They are tears of a just one; not tears for sins committed. How much better to say to God that one loves Him. How precious the tears of those who know no consolation because the Beloved of their hearts, seen behind the trellis, has all of a sudden been taken from their sight. And the Beloved was so taken away for many more years.

Divine Providence led her parents to send their daughter to a boarding school at Vans.

Marie Victoire was at this time seventeen years of age. That is beyond the age to begin such schooling. But yesterday is not today. Perhaps God led her to Vans that she might there hear a word, receive a sign. The smallest thing counts in the life of the elect. Bossuet says that the strokes of God have their counter strokes, which carry far. Marie Victoire departed from Le Mas.

This was the first separation.

II. The Meeting

THE DIRECTRESS of the boarding school, Mlle. Castanier, was a former Ursuline. A crown of martyrdom, such as her Sisters of Orange won, had been all but hers. Only the death of Robespierre had robbed her of that boon she so desired.[1]

Free again, this grave woman yearned to give to young souls something of the fire which burned within her. It is a common saying that one who has escaped death experiences a strong renewal of life. Such renewal God gave to Mlle. Castanier. She founded an educational institution and named it after Saint Joseph. The title "Educational Institution" is somewhat pretentious. We must not think it was like the boarding schools of our day. Life therein was like that of a closely united family, and had a very intense religious atmosphere. All else was secondary.

To this woman, once condemned to the scaffold, her parents entrusted their daughter, Marie Victoire. They could not have chosen a better means of planting within her young, innocent soul the seeds of strength, of courage, of heroism. Vans, it will be seen, had reason to be included in the divine plans.

We have no record of her years at this school. That of course does not prove they were fruitless. Who hears the slow mounting of the sap behind the bark? The silences of life have their usefulness. Days most obscure may be the most fruitful days of one's life.

Towards the end of March, 1825, M. Couderc came to Vans. "I took my daughter back," he tells us, "that she might help in the work of a mission which the priests of La Louvesc were to open. It was the first time since the Revolution that a mission was preached in our village, and I thought that Marie Victoire ought to be there." M. Couderc did not know how truthfully he spoke. Marie Victoire ought to be at Sablières because the hour of that meeting designed from all eternity by God had sounded. The day was approaching when the two divine instruments, the two founders of the great institution of the Cenacle, without knowing it, were to meet. Each advanced to the providential meeting by his and her separate road of duty.

Two centuries previous it was likewise appointed that the Bishop of Geneva should go to preach a Lenten course of sermons at Dijon and meet there the Baroness de Chantal. Saint Francis de Sales, attracted by this woman in black who sat in front of him while he preached, later asked Monsignor Frémiot: "Who is that widow who sits in front of the pulpit and who is so attentive?"

During the mission at Sablières, one of the three missionaries was led to ask the name of that young girl who was always so attentive to his sermons. She was then twenty years of age.

Surprising would it have been if God at that moment had raised for him the veil concealing the future, and revealed in France, England, Belgium, Italy, Holland, Switzerland, North and South America the convents with their many religious who would call him Founder, and her, this young girl, their first Mother.

* * *

John Peter Stephen Terme was the name of this missionary sent by God to Marie Victoire. Originally from Ardèche, he had for ten years past been curate at a little village called Aps. There his active zeal brought together a group of religious who devoted themselves to rural instruction. Active, zealous, enterprising, daring, Father Terme gave credit to Providence for everything. This last is, we believe, the most characteristic trait of his character. The holy priest lived altogether in the supernatural. What matters it, then, if human prudence had no part in him, if he pushed himself to the extreme of daring, if he spurned the wisdom of earth? God loves to put aside such wisdom. More than once He did so, when He made this curé, so adversely criticized by his confrères, the founder of two religious congregations.

The Bishop of Viviers came to him and entrusted him with the charge of the pilgrimage in honor of Saint John Francis Regis to La Louvesc, together with the task of evangelizing the surrounding country. Thus the play of secondary causes led him to Sablières in 1825.

We know nothing of the meeting of these two souls destined to sanctify themselves in accomplishing the one work. Yet it is easy to visualize the scene.

Marie Victoire found in this preacher a man of God. To him she opened her heart. "For some years now I have wished to be a religious. My father refuses his permission. I do not feel myself drawn to any particular order." The missionary answered with his customary decisiveness: "Go to Aps. I will give you a class of little ones to be instructed."

When he left Sablières, Father Terme thought he had found a most desirable teacher for his schools. For some time, God left him in that holy delusion. Providence is not often in a hurry. When the hour sounds, the Divine One passing along the borders of the Lake of Genesareth, will point out to the simple fisherman that only by casting the net on the other side of the boat will he draw in the miraculous draught.

III. Sister Claire

IN SPITE of the departure of the Founder, who had been called to head the pilgrimage of La Louvesc, the little novitiate at Aps continued to do well.

Most of the merit for that belongs to Sister Claire. Even when she was very young she had wished to give herself to God, but her invalided father claimed her care. She remained in the world, dividing her time between attending her father and instructing the very little ones of a baby class at the Convent of the Presentation. Her young protégés would call her nothing but Sister Claire. The name stuck to her. When Father Terme met her at Saint-Andéol, by that name this humble and generous-hearted woman was introduced to him. A few hours afterwards the missionary had decided what she was to do. "Nothing holds you now, since your father is dead. It is necessary that you take charge of my community of religious teachers." And so it happened. The new superior brought to Aps the rules and customs of the Presentation. Can one forget a page that he has loved? The newborn, unpretentious congregation took the name of "Teaching Sisters." [1] The zeal of Father Terme picked out candidates on almost every mission he preached. So there was no lack of subjects.

A Great and Humble Soul

It is told how one day Sister Claire was informed that twelve novices would arrive. Great anxiety resulted within the convent, for there were not enough beds for them. In great haste a sufficient number were purchased; this Apostolic College, of a decidedly new kind, arrived, and the convent was able to take care of them, as the ardent missionary had told them it would be.[2]

But the difference between the twelve Apostles and these twelve novices was that, of the Apostles only one went away; of the novices only one remained. That one was Marie Victoire Couderc.

How had she been able to leave Le Mas? Only with great difficulty. As soon as the mission at Sablières had closed, the young daughter had repeated her request for permission to be a religious. Again she was refused; and she had to submit. But Father Terme would never admit he was defeated. Some months later, having to journey to a neighboring village, he said to M. Couderc: "Give me Marie Victoire; I wish to make her a religious." Again M. Couderc refused. The poor child begged eagerly, saying that her prayers would bring blessings upon the family. But her father would not listen to reason. Finally after many months, the gentle pleading of the mother won from him a halting consent—so halting that, fearful lest he withdraw it, Marie Victoire hurriedly packed and left the next day. The record tells us that M. Couderc was unwilling to give any dowry to his daughter. She came in poverty. Father Terme was to have no regrets for having received this novice. She, like the disciples of the Cenacle, possessed nothing but her love of prayer. That January day whereon with her small bundle of clothes she entered the novitiate planted the seed that brought salvation to many souls.

Sister Claire received her with open arms and she soon outdistanced all her companions. "Power is at the source," said Lacordaire. This is not the place to show how this truth applied, nor to pay tribute to Sister Claire, to whom God had confided the moulding of one of His chosen. But Sister Claire was the hidden source whence came the great flood and she should never be forgotten in the reading of this history. All religious, both men and women, love to ascribe credit to novice master or mistress for the greater part of the supernatural life which they possess. At least there are none who do not recall with emotion the first lessons of sanctity received on the morning of their new life. As the years pass, they instinctively return to those lessons, seeking to breathe through the memory of them a purer air; to invigorate themselves by dwelling again on those first fervors.

Marie Victoire some years afterwards wrote thus of Sister Claire: "Everyone admired her modesty and her humility." She adds in parentheses—"I speak of what I have seen." Was not the deep humility of the Foundress of the Cenacle child of the humility of this very simple woman? Was it not because she had seen Sister Claire efface self

that Sister Marie Victoire, afterwards Mother
Thérèse, would seek, desire, love, even to the day
of her death, to take the last place?

Moreover, Father Terme gave the same instructions as the mistress of novices. A word of his that
has never yet been forgotten by his children is one
he gave to the novices at Aps: "You must be so
unassuming that the whole world may walk over
you." To be unassuming: that was the great lesson
that Sister Marie Victoire received in her novitiate.
That was also without doubt the light whereby
God illumined her soul on Easter Monday, March
27, 1826, when Bishop Bonnel, successor to Bishop
Molin, came to give the habit to this young postulant.

That morning, Marie Victoire received the
name of Sister Thérèse. The name was a forecasting and a program. A forecasting, for Thérèse
Couderc, like that other Teresa, the great lover of
Jesus, was also to be a foundress. The program was
to be one of love humiliated. One of the leading
mottoes of Saint John of the Cross was "Lord, to
be despised for Thy sake!"

Her mother, at least we may believe so, was
present at her reception of the habit. To this holy
woman was due this newly made religious. Her
prayers, her example, and particularly the triumph
she had won over the heart of her husband, gave
her reason to be proud of her work.

But she did not know that in her farewell embrace of the young Marie Victoire, whom the

Bishop had named Thérèse, she had given to her the last kiss on this earth.[3]

Some little while later Madame Couderc died.

And now the novice with plaited hair lives her simple hidden life. Of this formative period we will say nothing except that, providentially, she was not sent any longer, as so many of her fellow novices were, to teach in the village schools. Nor need this surprise us. Marie Victoire had come to Aps not to learn to teach a class of children, but to receive there her first lesson in humility. That is why the Religious of the Cenacle joyfully recall this novitiate of their Foundress and why for every one of them the saintly novice mistress of Mother Thérèse is held in venerable and venerated memory—as a pastel somewhat faded of one of long ago.

IV. The Virgin's Smile

THE CENACLE was born of the love of purity. Such a fact should be no cause for surprise. It was most fitting that this religious order, destined in the plans of God to honor the life of the Holy Virgin, between the Ascension and Pentecost, should shine forth upon the world as the smile of Our Blessed Mother.

The very simple story of this mysterious birth is as follows:

Father Terme did much good at La Louvesc and was well beloved by its inhabitants. But one thing deeply tormented him. The innkeepers, as the number of pilgrims greatly increased, frequently lodged in the same rooms persons of both sexes. The holy priest dreaded to think of God being offended. One day, as he was offering Mass over the tomb of Saint Francis Regis, the thought came to him that if he could establish a house for the women pilgrims, many scandals would be avoided. But would not such an effort tempt Providence? Where could the necessary money be found? In the meanwhile a Jesuit Father came to La Louvesc. Father Terme told him of his ambitions. The Jesuit Father, a man of years and experience, seconded Father Terme's plans. "The project certainly comes from God," he said. "Do all that you can to carry it out as soon as possible. Above all, do not be discouraged by the difficulties with which you will meet. You will not be without them."

The Society of Jesus has taken a leading part in the history of the Cenacle. It blessed its cradle; it foresaw its trials of the morrow. When the hour of its tribulation sounded, it was there to utter the word of comfort. To it Mother Thérèse ever turned for strength.

A short time after the departure of the Jesuit Father, Father Terme went to interview his

Bishop. Seated in the corner of the diligence which took him to Viviers, the good missionary thought only of how he could at once obtain permission from Bishop Bonnel to build the desired house.

He almost failed in his endeavor. The Bishop's council was of a mind to refuse authorization. "Father Terme is a fanatic," they said, "a dreamer. Wisdom dictates that we should distrust his impulses."

Thanks to God, the Bishop went over their heads. The missionary returned to La Louvesc with permission to go forward with his project.

A hundred meters from the public square of the village, on the right of the road which leads to the fountain of Saint Francis Regis, stood an old house formerly owned by the Society of Jesus. Saint Francis Regis lodged there, it is said, on his way from Tournon to Le Puy. The property on which it stood measured several hundred meters square. The price asked was ten thousand francs. Father Terme, besides owing many bills, had but two hundred francs in his possession. Yet he bought the property. After all, he acted in the name of a rich Master. That Master, when the time came, would give him the money necessary.

His reasoning was perfectly logical for one who lives fully in the supernatural. Therein, as we have said, Father Terme dwelt. That also is why, being simply told by a confrère that he was not putting up a large enough building, he did not hesitate to change the plans although the work was far advanced. As was just, the contractor asked increased payment. But such requests did not stop the missionary. God blessed His humble builder. The money necessary to pay the workers was never lacking. If there were agonizing hours, those hours were followed by a Magnificat of gratitude to that Providence which time and again came with the unexpected aid.

It is here we should speak of two devoted souls whom God led to aid His servant.

At La Louvesc there was much talk about the new house being built. The innkeepers spoke against it; others praised it without reserve. Among the admirers of Father Terme were two devout young women, both of whom bore names loved and respected throughout the countryside—Françoise Blache and Nanette Buisson.

These two good Christians went one day to the missionary and said: "We come to offer you all of our savings—two hundred francs. You may use our house to lodge women pilgrims while you are waiting for the completion of your own. Indeed, we ourselves are at the service of your work." Generosity could go no further.

Father Terme accepted their entire offer. The two hundred francs would pay for the registering with the notary of the record of sale; the offered house would receive the young women on pilgrimage; and as to Françoise and Nanette—well, Father Terme gave them, during his absences, supervision of his work-yards.

It is proper we mention these chosen souls who very soon afterwards joined the novitiate at Aps.[1] God, Who had used them in the building of the first house of the Cenacle, did not permit both of them to die in the community of the Cenacle. Guided by the Holy Spirit, Nanette Buisson devoted herself to another foundation of Father Terme and became Superior General of the Sisters of Saint Regis.

What matters it? The two works of the holy Founder are divine: each one came from his heart. The self-consecration of Nanette Buisson, in religion Sister Stanislaus, can never be forgotten. This rugged worker of the first hours gave not in vain of her sweat and her fatigue in helping to erect the walls of the birth-place of the Cenacle. Her labor has merited to be a source of benedictions, as is everything that is pure and good, and the Cenacle continues to be ever grateful to her.

V. The Three Elect

BUILDING WAS not the greatest problem. When the roof was on and the walls plastered, it was necessary to put a soul into the lifeless body of this house. Father Terme pondered as to which one of his daughters at Aps was to his own image

and likeness. It seemed to him absolutely necessary that the superior at La Louvesc should be
selected from the novices there. But this difficulty
at once presented itself: Aps was the mother house
of a congregation established for conducting rural
schools. La Louvesc was without question tend-
ing towards a different kind of work.

Perhaps it would have been the wiser course not
to have tried to combine these two very different
sources, and to have founded with a different per-
sonnel this work which Saint Francis Regis had
suggested to Father Terme. Had this been done,
more than one trial would have been prevented,
but we certainly would never have had Mother
Thérèse. She would have been simply Sister
Thérèse, and the teacher of a class all her life.

Let us bless God, then, because once more
Father Terme lacked human wisdom, and brought
those religious from the novitiate at Aps to live at
La Louvesc. The three selected were: Sister Agnes,
Sister Thérèse and Sister Regis.[1]

The Founder at first wished to entrust the
charge of the new house to Sister Thérèse. He
hesitated because of her age. She was but twenty-
one. He finally appointed Sister Agnes, who was
forty years old, as head of the little community.[2]

Then one day, the public bus brought the three
religious; and they descended from it at the fountain square. Father Terme welcomed them with
his habitual kindness. He escorted them to their

new lodgings. And what lodgings! Saint Francis of Assisi would have recognized them for his own.

The written record of Mother Thérèse enables us to make those heroic hours alive again. "When we entered the house at La Louvesc we found but one finished room—the kitchen. Our only means of getting to the four or five small cells on the first floor—our dormitory—was a ladder. The walls were so recently plastered that one fairly breathed lime. Many who showed interest in our welfare begged us not to stay in the house. 'You will get ill,' said the Countess de Clavières. 'What matters it,' we answered. 'Why should we not abandon ourselves to Providence and get ill, if that is necessary, for this work of Providence?' But happily the good God took care of us. We healthy ones did not fall ill. Providence seemed to bless our poverty which in very truth was extreme. For our table service we had but four spoons and four forks of iron or pewter."

It was necessary that we quote these actual words of Mother Thérèse. In themselves they express something of the simplicity of those first days when the sisters lived without thought of the morrow, without even seeking to know where God would lead this infant work.

Father Terme later recalled that at that time kneeling in a chapel of the Blessed Virgin he felt himself urged to make this prayer: "One thing suffices me—I ask only that I may accomplish the work God has destined for me; I do not seek to know what that work may be." [3] Rarely was a prayer more fully heard. He and his daughters labored without knowing just exactly what God wished. If he took it upon himself to say that he had done no more than to quit the world and become a hotel keeper, his faith quickly repudiated this defeatist thought. And the good Father, as they called him in this new house, gave himself entirely to his beloved Providence.

On a day in 1827, the very year they came to La Louvesc, Father Terme got the strange idea of giving his daughters a different habit. Just at that time a Jesuit Father journeyed through the village. He presided at the ceremony. A simple detail this, unimportant to such as do not look deeply into things; a significant coincidence to those who ponder on the designs of God. At every important date in the life of the Cenacle one will find present a Father of the Society of Jesus.

In the habit chosen by Father Terme the color violet prevailed. The reason for this is that violet was the distinguishing color of those who vowed themselves to Saint Francis Regis.

The story is told that this good Jesuit, who knew little of the technical details of the habits of religious women, announced to the assembled people that at the ceremony: [4] "The Sisters of Saint Regis will this evening receive a habit with a violet veil and black wimple." The wimple was never black. The people of La Louvesc, very much puzzled,

me in crowds, as the record tells us, to see these
ligious so costumed. Many were the smiles when
ey saw that the black wimple was white, and the
olet veil was black.

And now an unlooked-for event happened
hich advanced the work of God. Sister Agnes,
iece of Father Barrial, the curé of Plagnal, was
eremptorily recalled by her uncle to take charge
the school in his village. The good Father
erme owed too much to Father Barrial, who had
ded him to become a priest, to refuse his request.
ster Agnes left La Louvesc.[5] At the same time,
ster Thérèse, up to then assistant and mistress
novices, became superior.

The light was taken from under the bushel. It
one for ten years.

Of these ten years we are about to tell. After
eing all the fruits with which they were filled,
e asks himself how was it possible not to have
alized sooner what a treasure Mother Thérèse
as.

The merchant in pearls of the Gospel ex-
anged all his false pearls in order to secure a
al one.

At La Louvesc, Providence permitted the barter-
g of a real pearl for a false one.

PART TWO
The Light

VI. The First Gleam

SOME DAYS after her appointment as superior, Sister Thérèse received the following note from Father Terme: "Although you think yourself wholly unworthy, remember that you hold the place of Christ Jesus. Do Him honor, therefore, and respect His authority. Be strong with His strength: powerful with His power. Do not allow any article of the Rule to be set aside. Be faithful to the devotional exercises: let no one neglect them." Such was the program to follow. Contemporaneous records tell us that the young superior never departed from this ideal, so vigorously expressed. "Then," writes a religious of La Louvesc, "Sister Thérèse was named superior. She won the love of her sisters by her extreme humility, her scrupulous exactitude in keeping the Holy Rule, and her exemplary fidelity in the practice of obedience.

"Lover of prayer, she was the first in chapel, the last to leave."

Could ideal and reality be in more perfect accord? We will endeavor now to see the young superior at work; we will endeavor particularly to grasp that one moment when her heart made a wonderful discovery and she became in truth the Foundress of the Cenacle.

The House of Saint Regis, such was the name given to this new dwelling, counted only three or four religious. Shortly after the departure of Sister Agnes, the community became more numerous, since Father Terme decided to transfer the novitiate from Aps to La Louvesc.

The latter, therefore, became the motherhouse, and Sister Thérèse, Superior General of all the schools scattered throughout the countryside. But the life of the sisters of this House of Saint Regis was totally different in the winter months from what it was in summer.

In winter time there were no pilgrimages. But a splendid opportunity offered itself for the sisters to go into the mountains to teach catechism, to give general school instruction. In this they never failed. Under the strong rule of the young superior the evangelization of the poor was carried out in spite of cold and snow. Many edifying instances of the courage of these religious might be cited. One which is still frequently retold by the daughters of Father Terme is as follows:

Father Savin, co-laborer with Father Terme, preached one day at Saint-Agrève. He was at that time informed of a small parish, some short distance from the village, called Saint-Romain-le-Désert. It was utterly abandoned. The church, the rectory, the school, all had been closed these many years because no priest was there.

Moved by this story of extreme need, Father Savin secured from the Bishop of Viviers permission to use his own salary to make the necessary repairs. He then asked Father Terme for two religious to conduct the school.

Father Terme [1] was happy to be able to render this service to his co-laborer. He went to the House of Saint Regis, called together the community, made known the request that had been made of him, and asked a favorable response from that young, zealous group.

The nature of the response could scarcely be doubted. All except one begged to be chosen. That one was Sister Joséphine, and she oddly enough was also the one whom Father Terme in his own mind had selected. The good Father was pleased at the almost unanimous willingness to undertake the sacrifice, but he made no decision then. The next day he sent an order to Sister Thérèse to the effect that she should assign for the work at Saint-Romain-le-Désert, Sister Joséphine and a postulant, Rosalie Nicolas. Sister Joséphine was convinced that she should make known her mind to her superior, and the latter as soon as she knew it did not hesitate to confer with Father Terme.

It would be natural to expect that he would stand by the formal order given. But Father Terme did nothing of the sort. Mother Thérèse knew how to convince the Founder, and he named Sister Regis in place of Sister Joséphine.

A few weeks at Saint-Romain sufficed to undermine the strength of Sister Regis. She returned to La Louvesc and Sister Joséphine left to join Rosalie Nicolas.

To describe what these two poor women had to endure would be quite impossible. On Sunday they went to Saint-Agrève to assist at Mass, for the priest did not come to Saint-Romain except once every three weeks.

Leaving their house at daybreak, they had to walk until ten o'clock, oftentimes making their way through snow drifts as high as the knee. Fasting, that they might receive Holy Communion, drenched, shivering with the cold, these poor children of Mother Thérèse on arrival found no other comfort than a foot stove prepared for them by Mademoiselle du Grail, a devout woman of the parish. She would also give them seats in her pew and after Mass serve them breakfast—in haste always, for as soon as possible these two self-sacrificing sisters were obliged to return to Saint-Romain to give instruction to the women and the young girls.

All this would have been trial enough, if the necessities of life had not been lacking. Indeed, they were time and again without enough food to satisfy their hunger.

It is told how a child one day bringing some fagots to the sisters asked for a small piece of bread. The cupboards were empty. It was necessary to borrow the bread; and the bread was faithfully returned as soon as Providence made it possible.

At another time, they were without water. To obtain drinking water they had to melt snow brought into the kitchen.

Once the two good women were shut in by the freezing cold and they had to secure the services of a boy, who made his way through a tunnel of ice to care for the sanctuary lamp.[2]

If the glory of the disciple be the glory of the master, the heroism of these two holy daughters lost in these fastnesses of snow must in great part be accredited to her who knew how to inspire them. The lessons taught by Sister Thérèse were lessons of the power and love of God. They who willingly lived, forgotten for months, without protection against hunger and cold, must indeed have loved God very much.

* * *

When the fair weather came, the atmosphere about the Saint Regis House changed completely.

On Saturday afternoon at four o'clock veritable caravans of pilgrims began to make their way to the public square of La Louvesc. At six o'clock the church was filled with the faithful, the confessionals besieged.

For two, sometimes three days, the religious hospice of Father Terme was given over to a noisy, exacting and oftentimes ill-behaved crowd. At least, that is what a notation of Sister Thérèse tells us: "The women were so numerous that we had not beds for one quarter of them: but it was impossible to refuse any, and so we were forced to put mattresses in the hallways. Moreover, a great number of them were so ill-behaved that it was impossible to keep them in anything like order." The superior would have oftentimes preferred that her daughters were at Saint-Romain-le-Désert. For six months it was impossible for her to maintain at Saint Regis the observances of the religious life. Sister Thérèse states so in terms that admit of no doubt: "It was," she says, "an impossible situation for those who desired to live the religious life."

Anxious, troubled, the young superior appealed to God, and God answered her. In a moment, a sudden light illumined her at prayer. It showed her the remedy for the evil.

"Give no lodging to anyone who does not agree to make a novena or a triduum in honor of Saint Regis."

With characteristic insight her own soul quickly and fully grasped what it had thus received from the light of heaven. But how could Father Terme be led to change his own plans? She reflected, she prayed, and then courageously she faced the holy Founder.

What she afterwards wrote warrants us in believing that the first interviews were far from welcome.

"I succeeded at last in having the good Father see," she says, "that to lead the religious life under the circumstances was impossible." But he would not at first consent. His objection was no doubt based on the fear that the scandals caused by the practices of the innkeepers would recur because few of the women would be willing to stay in the house for nine or even three days and spend that time in prayer. They would go to the inn. The young superior had suffered so much from the existing situation that she answered that the vocation of souls called by God to the religious life ought also to be considered: that one religious leading a truly supernatural life could protect an entire region.

To make the story brief, she won her cause and in a short while the house was transformed. "From that time forth the situation was entirely different." No longer were the corridors crowded; nor the hallways filled with mattresses; nor the dining-room filled to overflowing. The shouting throughout the house, the loud laughter in the bedrooms, ceased.

"Every guest at Saint Regis was in quietude, making either a triduum or a novena." [3]

There is something in those lines of the joy expressed by a military commander when he sends a message of victory. Indeed it was a victory that

Sister Thérèse had won. It was more than a victory, but she did not know it. One more ascending step and we will have the Cenacle. When the novena and the triduum will have become the retreat, and when during the retreat the Spiritual Exercises of Saint Ignatius will be preached, the work will have been completed.

So it is that to the young superior of La Louvesc the Cenacle owes that first idea from which it took birth. Her love of recollection, of silence, of regularity in the religious life brought forth from her heart the saving remedy. In this sense, as in so many others, she is truly the Foundress.

The grain is planted in the furrow; nothing will prevent its growth.

The first light has broken through the darkness. The sun itself is not far off.

VII. The Exercises of Saint Ignatius

AT VALS, a few kilometers from the town of Le Puy, the Jesuit Fathers have a scholasticate —a house of study for their young religious. Vals is a name well known, at least to all those interested in The Apostleship of Prayer. In that house

Part Two: *The Light*

at Vals the great work was initiated by Fathers
Gautrelet and Ramière.

To that same house the Cenacle is also, in a way,
connected, because of what follows here.

Father Terme was always devoted to the Order
of Saint Ignatius. Whether it was that his ardent
nature, impetuous as a torrent, felt the need of
severe discipline, or that he desired this discipline
because of his love of sacrifice, the thought of becoming a Jesuit ever remained with him. It need
not surprise us, then, to learn that Father Terme
came, during the year 1827 or 1828 (the exact year
is doubtful), to Vals and entered into a retreat under the direction of one of the Fathers.[1]

For the first time he read the book of the Exercises. Therein God awaited him. Therein he saw
the clear, brilliant light. The logic of Saint Ignatius, the ardent love of the Saint for the King
of the Kingdom, his desire to save the vast multitudes who were rushing headlong to perdition, his
self-abnegation which drove him to the third degree of humility—all these were fully grasped by
the soul of Father Terme.

He carefully copied with his own hand during
that retreat all the pages of the book, and even
the smallest note which the Father gave him for
his reading. This eagerness, this importance which
he gave to even the smallest parts of the Exercises,
reveals to us that this ardent soul was pursued by
the thought of some great project, for the fulfil-

ment of which the book of Saint Ignatius would
serve as a guide.

And this was the case. From the time when Sister Thérèse had secured his consent that everyone
stopping at the Saint Regis House should make
at least a triduum, Father Terme saw both the
transformation effected in the lives of the religious
themselves and the good work done for the souls
of the guests by these days of recollection.

At his first contact with Saint Ignatius he felt
himself deeply impressed. One statement of the
author, above all, had struck him forcibly. It was
that where the Saint speaks of the superiority of
private retreats, because in such retreats it is possible to adapt the great truths of religion to the
capacity of each one, and without too much talking thereon. "It is necessary," says Saint Ignatius,
"to leave the creature with his Creator."

Father Terme further felt himself enlightened
from on high to change into retreats both the
triduum and the novenas asked for by Sister
Thérèse, and to arrange to have the Exercises of
Saint Ignatius given to those who would come on
pilgrimage. Why should not his daughters become,
in such a holy ministry, humble but devoted co-
laborers with the Fathers of the Society of Jesus?

When Father Terme left Vals, having completed
his eight days of retreat, he had made up his mind
to establish an order of religious women devoted
to the work of retreats.

Once he realized that a thing was to be done,

this holy Founder was not accustomed to permit himself to be embarrassed by the difficulties inherent in its execution. In his own mind he saw the whole work clearly.

As soon as he left the bus which carried him to La Louvesc, without taking the time even to stop at his own house, he went immediately to the community. They were at supper, so he went straight to the refectory. Everyone stood, out of respect.

"I have some news to tell you," he said. "But since it will affect some of you very much, I would ask you to continue your supper. I will make it known to you when you have finished."

In spite of the suggestion not to hurry, they ate hastily in order the sooner to know this news which awaited them. After they had finished, this is what Father Terme said: "I give you notice that four of you will this evening go into retreat—Sister Thérèse, Sister Joséphine, Sister Marie and Sister Saint Joseph."

All the sisters looked at one another in astonishment. They showed no great enthusiasm. Realizing this, Father Terme added in a tone of authority: "Let no one ponder over what I have said: let no one utter a word on the subject—either for or against. If anyone does say a word, she will have to account for it to me." [2]

The first retreat of the future Cenacle did not have much of the atmosphere of peace about it. Nevertheless deep fervor characterized it and that was imparted by Father Terme himself. It is inter-

esting to learn the impressions made upon Sister
Thérèse by this introduction to the Spiritual Exercises at Saint Regis House.

"Father Terme gave us the method of Saint Ignatius, and some small pages for meditation which
merely indicated the subject, for there were no
more than two written lines. With these pages, he
gave us our retreat. It was the first time we made
a retreat according to the method of Saint Ignatius,
a method of which we had, up to that time, never
heard a word. And I may truly say that we followed it without comprehending it. It was in vain
that we read this method which Father Terme had
recommended so highly; we did not understand it
in the least until it was finally explained to us." [3]

That appealing page enables us to realize how
these religious women first stammered a language
which afterwards was to become their mother
tongue.

These points for meditation, given in one or two
lines, these notes, additions, rules for the discerning of spirits, the different methods of prayer,
these general and particular examinations of conscience, gave naught to their souls but an impression of confusion. So they thought they were
dreaming when on the morning the retreat closed
they heard Father Terme command them to give
the Spiritual Exercises to the guests then making
a novena.

The poor bewildered sisters objected that they
did not sufficiently understand the book of Saint

Ignatius. They could but say, as Joan of Arc to the heavenly voices: "We know not A from B." But Father Terme was no more conciliating than the Archangel: "Go and do it, daughters of God," he said. "Go and do it." And all the daughters of God obeyed.

Mother Thérèse herself, distraught, trembling, ran to the chapel to prostrate herself before the Blessed Sacrament and implore Our Lord to come to her aid.

God has included in that prayer all those who as children of Mother Thérèse have been called upon to exercise the same apostolate and who having known fear have in like manner turned unto Him. Who among the Religious of the Cenacle required for the first time to give the Spiritual Exercises, has not felt some of the agonies experienced by her Mother?

Mother Thérèse, strengthened by her humble prayer, obeyed from her heart. We need not, however, think that in the meanwhile God lifted all her fears.

"We did not dare," she wrote, "use the word 'retreat,' but we recommended certain books for reading and for meditation, so that the guests should more profitably spend the time of the novena."

It seems that the good country people of the Ardèche did not allow themselves to be taken in by this innocent subterfuge. "We do not know how to meditate," they gruffly declared. And the sisters answered: "To meditate—but that is simply to think about religion. You know, don't you, how to think about your business matters? . . ."

They began to think about religion, and—to the great astonishment of the sisters, who thought they had disguised their designs—they published it all about that retreats were given at Saint Regis.

The news, however, did not displease the people of the surrounding territory, for soon the number of retreatants grew so large that Mother Thérèse wrote: "We have not enough beds for them."

Visibly then, Providence willed this new work, and Providence came to the aid of the young superior.

One day she received a gift of two thousand francs; another day, three thousand. A farmer came and offered ten thousand francs for those extensions which were most needed.

Mother Thérèse could not restrain her joy, pondering how different the house was from the noisy hotel of yesterday. "We were moved to admiration at the fervor with which they made the Exercises."

This time the Cenacle was well founded. By a delicate balancing, nothing short of providential, both Founder and Foundress played his and her part in this divine work: Mother Thérèse by insisting upon novenas and triduums; Father Terme in replacing the novenas and triduums by the Spiritual Exercises of Saint Ignatius.

* * *

Part Two: *The Light*

As this new work increasingly developed, the question presented itself to all: what was to be done about the schools?

Father Terme, embarrassed by the success of the retreat work, anxiously considered what his decision should be.

Should he pilot both works, or should he give himself entirely to one—the work of retreats?

It seems that at first he was inclined to have his daughters engaged in two separate apostolic labors. That conclusion may at least be drawn from a letter he wrote to Pauline Jaricot, Foundress of the Propagation of the Faith.

Pauline Jaricot herself had also thought of the plan of giving retreats. After she made known her thought to Father Terme, he wrote her the following letter:

MY DEAR SISTER IN JESUS CHRIST:

I would ask you to consider the matter with our Saviour and weigh it in the light which He will give you. You wish to have retreats conducted. So do I. I have no means. You have sacrificed all your resources. But if it be pleasing to Jesus and Mary, I offer you, in the name of the holy Virgin, the house at La Louvesc. You need select only those sisters who will be judged useful in the giving of retreats by our Jesuit Fathers. I charge myself with the obligation of withdrawing the others and of employing them elsewhere. I could, perhaps, in this latter way employ some of yours. As regards the habit, I agree to accept, and the sisters will accept, everything you decide thereon with the Jesuit Fathers.

As regards the Rule, it is that of Saint Ignatius, and since it is not a new Rule, I do not think the Archbishop will place any obstacles in the way of adopting it.

If this plan is carried out, I promise you a great number of vocations, of subjects distinguished for their piety, their education, their talents. Money will not be lacking, I am certain.

On the other hand, we must not deceive ourselves: it is necessary for us to have the aid of the Jesuit Fathers.

Yes, we have those who are able to direct the retreatants, but we have not those who are able to give the Exercises to women individually. It is, however, precisely this individual instruction that the true Ignatian method demands. Did not Saint Ignatius intend that each soul should have placed before it that which is suited to its special need? But this individual instruction of women should be given by women. Such women can be found. The young persons to whom God has given a taste for such a vocation are already numerous.

I believe it a great part of the designs of God that you recommend this matter to the Hearts of Jesus and of Mary.

Pray well concerning these things and have your prayers include me.

TERME.

Part Two: *The Light*

This letter holds in germ the separation of the sisters conducting schools and the sisters conducting retreats. Father Terme at that time seems to have visualized two distinct sections of his Congregation: one devoting itself to the schools, the other devoting itself to the giving of the Exercises. Some little time afterwards the plan developed still further in his mind.

The work of conducting retreats frankly took precedence over that of conducting schools. This fact of precedence stands out clearly in the Constitutions wherein he wrote: "This work (the work of conducting retreats) is our principal, essential work." On that passage Mother Thérèse later commented: "Among the works which Father Terme founded, the principal one is that of conducting retreats. It is he who conceived that work; he who strove to realize it."

Father Terme subsequently took a further step forward. Towards the end of his life, the work of retreats became for him the sole work to be followed. In his will he speaks only of his daughters of the retreat work, whom he confides to the Bishop and to the Society of Jesus. If he had had the intention of remaining the master pilot of the two orders, would he have neglected to mention his other daughters? His mind at first was: the two works to be equally stressed: then the retreat work as the essential work: finally the retreat work as the sole work.

Man may propose, but God disposes.

That unity which, through his humility perhaps, the holy man seems to have decided upon, was not permitted to be by Divine Providence. Besides the work of conducting retreats, some of the daughters of Father Terme were to continue, to the great profit of souls, the work of conducting schools. This proves the richness of the sap able to give nourishment to the two branches.

Whatever be the successive developments in the plans of the Founder, the documents we have cited show the utter senselessness of the accusation brought at one time against Mother Thérèse— that she had established a new community and that she was no daughter of Father Terme.[4]

No indeed. The two branches sprang from the one stem. That enemy of mankind, the sower of tares, will never succeed in dividing the children of the one same father.

VIII. The Last Years of Father Terme

VALS SO deeply impressed Father Terme, that he would not think of having the Exercises of Saint Ignatius given to his daughters save by a Father of the Society of Jesus. The art of giving the Exercises of Saint Ignatius is a difficult one. A

Jesuit himself makes the entire Exercises twice:
once during his novitiate; a second time during
the third year of his probationship, before his last
vows. We may add that he lives in their atmosphere, he is nourished by them every day. We do
no injustice to anyone when we state that by reason
of his vocation he is better fitted than others to
wield this weapon.

Father Terme, then, asked for a Jesuit. One
came from the house at Avignon. His name was
Father Délage.

The date of this retreat is uncertain. Some place
it in 1828; others, in 1830. The difference in time
is great, but happily in the absence of precise information as to date, we are well informed as to
the event itself. It was of supreme importance.
During the retreat Father Délage proposed that
these religious take the vows. Up to that time none
of the daughters of Father Terme had taken any
vows; neither at Aps nor La Louvesc had the ir-
revocable consecration been made.

An incident occurred in connection with the
vows that was, to say the least, original. When
Father Délage stated that only the fervent religious should ask thus to bind themselves to God,
no one answered his appeal. The Father thought
poorly of them because of this lack of eagerness.
He feared they were living too comfortably, and
he asked to be allowed to visit the bedrooms and
the dormitories. At sight of the unplastered walls,
full of holes as large as one's hand, of the poor

straw mattresses resting upon a board or the bare earth, he exclaimed: "But my bedroom is luxurious compared to yours and mine has no more than is absolutely necessary."

The Father then questioned Sister Thérèse. Her answer greatly edified him: "No one thinks herself worthy enough to meet the requirements of fervor which you laid down."

The ceremony of the vows was held in the room in which the retreats were given, and where a little temporary altar was built.

Sister Thérèse, who on that day and in that room took the title of "Mother," with some others judged worthy of consecrating themselves to God, pronounced her vows.

Father Délage preached. Whether he was truly inspired, or whether he just voiced his own conviction, the fact remains that, pointing to the altar, he declared: "This altar forecasts that which later you will have with you." He spoke of a new chapel. And he was not deceived: a beautiful chapel was built later in the Saint Regis House.[1]

On a May day in 1909 the coffin of Mother Thérèse will be taken from the cemetery of La Louvesc and placed in that chapel. It is there that the great and humble one will await that glory which we trust will be accorded her by the Church.

* * *

For the time being the community was renewed by its contact of eight days with Saint Ignatius.

PART TWO: *The Light*

With great fervor, it followed the discipline laid down by Father Terme: Hour of rising, half-past four; then meditation; at ten o'clock, spiritual reading—particular examen; one o'clock, visit to the tomb of Saint Regis; two o'clock, spiritual reading. In the evening, visit to the Blessed Sacrament, rosary, evening prayers, examen.

Every day at three o'clock Father Terme would come to explain the catechism.

At times they would go into the woods to gather fire-wood. On those days they took their meals wherever they chanced to be, and during the meals conversation was allowed; but complete silence was observed during work. It was not a rare thing for Father Terme to appear quite suddenly. . . . The holy Founder would sit upon a bundle of wood and just talk about the things of God.

There are Mother Thérèse and her handful of religious cutting branches, bundling and tying them. And there is Father Terme, a detached figure because of his black cassock against a background of white coifs, making holy by his words the rude labor of these workers.

This simple detail shows us also with what solicitude Father Terme cared for his daughters. Two incidents will show us that he never failed in maintaining religious discipline: he did not insist on it at one time and pass it by at another.

The first concerns a feast day of Saint Francis Regis, June 16th. Their desire to hear the panegyric on their patron saint led the religious to go to the church without having first put the house in order for the day. Father Terme, learning of this, notified Mother Thérèse that not one of the religious would be allowed to be present that evening at the parish devotions.[2] Another fault was still more severely punished. One day, soldiers, a band at their head, passed through the village. This was a rare sight for La Louvesc. The sisters sought places on the steps of the porch in order to see them go by. Informed of this, Father Terme came to give judgment. The sentence was:—not to mention other penances—eight days of silence. Truly, at La Louvesc nature was conquered, so grace made great headway. Under the strong impetus of the Founder, the little community gave an example of solid virtue. The development of this spiritual life Father Terme held to be more important than anything else. For that reason he decided to have the Blessed Sacrament in the house. The retreat hall was transformed into an oratory.[3] To have the Blessed Sacrament in their own house was an intimate, personal joy for all the sisters, for the devout Mother Thérèse in particular, who from that time began the habit, which she continued all her life, of spending many hours before the Tabernacle. In this chapel took place one of the last notable acts in the life of the Founder.

Father Terme was a man of original ideas. One day he called his daughters to the small oratory. When they had gathered, they saw the Father kneeling. "Join with me," he said very solemnly:

PART TWO: *The Light*

"In the name of the Most Holy, the Most Adorable Trinity, Father, Son and Holy Spirit, I, John Peter Stephen Terme, faithless servant of the Mother of my Jesus, before the most high, the most powerful, and august Queen of Angels and of men, the divine Mary, in presence of Saint Regis and of the whole court of heaven, humbly and sincerely acknowledge that the house at La Louvesc occupied by the Sisters of Saint Regis does not belong to me: that it is without reason that men believe that I am the owner. They do so, no doubt, because the bill of sale for this place and the surrounding land was made out in my name. But I hereby declare in presence of the court of heaven and under the Eyes of Jesus Christ, that it was not I who did the building; it was not my money that paid the laborers; that I do not even know how all this was done. I am surprised that such an extended plan was adopted. It was not my hand that traced it. I cannot understand how, without money, without resources of any kind, anyone had the hardihood to purchase such an expensive site, to gather together such material and in so great a quantity, to call to the yards so many laborers. And what I can even less understand is how all those workers were well paid, that they were content, that they even made a good profit. I must in very truth say that I not only had nothing, but I still owed much on the house at Aps. Who, then, built the house at La Louvesc known as Saint Regis? You but deceive yourselves, all you who imagine that it was the Abbé Terme of Plagnal. To speak the whole truth, I know of no man who built it, and frankly I believe men had nothing to do with it.

"Yes, O my God, there is every evidence that it is Thy work; every evidence that Thy Divine Providence built this house; that Thy Divine Providence feeds and clothes those who dwell therein. Indeed, the furniture they use, the habits they wear, the bread they eat, are as certainly gifts from Thy Hand as was the manna by which Thou didst feed Thy people for forty years in the desert. Even though it may be given all at one time instead of being given day by day, it is none the less miraculous, the bread which they eat here. O Mary, O my Mother, it is through thee that all these good things are given to us. Art not thou the Treasurer of heaven?

"I repeat my statement, O divine Queen, this house does not belong to me. It is thine. I feel I give thee a gift much soiled by my own free will. It is unworthy of thee, my good Mother. My gift merits refusal, and yet I hope it will be acceptable to thee. It will be so, my Mother, because thou couldst never see thy way to reject a house in which thy Jesus has willed to dwell. His Presence purifies all, and thou wilt not refuse to take as thy daughters the lowly children who enjoy the signal favor of living under one roof with Jesus, thy Son. Behold how thy Jesus suffers them to labor, just as He permits them to eat, to sleep, to enjoy recreation in the very house in which He Himself dwells. Yes, thou wilt receive them; thou wilt protect them; thou wilt save them from evil; thou wilt make them saints.

"If it is true that I am their Superior in the Faith and their Father in Jesus Christ, from this hour I constitute thee, I appoint thee their Superior General.

"I beseech thee to accept that office for the love of Jesus, for the glory of God the Father, of Whom thou art the well-beloved daughter, for the honor of the Holy Spirit, of Whom thou art the cherished spouse. Under thy heavenly rule, receive without exception all those who are at La Louvesc, as also those at Aps, at Mayres, at Plagnal, at Lespéron, at Lamastre, at Saint-Pal, at Valvignères. I give to thee and thou wilt accept with equal affection my beloved daughters who have come from Lyons, that they also may be thine always.

"To show that all my daughters embrace and will persevere in the profession of these truths, they place their signatures here with that of the lowest and the most unworthy of thy servants."

When Father Terme had finished reading, all the sisters with Mother Thérèse at their head, came forward and signed this act consecrating themselves to the Blessed Virgin.[4] They numbered ten: to these must be added the four daughters of Mlle. Pauline Jaricot, who had been sent from Lyons for the retreat work. This wholly original "act" made a profound impression on Mother

Thérèse. Six years later she was to recall the little chapel at La Louvesc, and at the feet of Notre-Dame d'Ay, on the eve of her great trials, she was to declare that the true superior of the Congregation was the Blessed Virgin.

This consecration of himself made by Father Terme took place shortly before his journey into eternity. Had the holy Founder some presentiment that his course was near its end? We may well believe so, for in the month of September of that same year he made his will.

Having committed his Congregation to the Blessed Virgin, he desired, humanly speaking, to give up everything. The terms of his will are as follows:

"In the name of the Most Holy Trinity, Father, Son and Holy Spirit, I the undersigned, John Peter Stephen Terme, priest, declare this present writing to be my last will:

"1. I pray God the Father, that by the merits of Jesus Christ His Divine Son, and by the power of the Holy Spirit, He deign to pardon my sins and receive me into His merciful bosom. I commend my soul to my Patron Saints, Saint John, Saint Peter, Saint Stephen, to my Guardian Angel and to the glorious Virgin Mary, my good Mother.

"2. I commend my dear daughters of the Retreat to their glorious Patron, Saint Regis, to the Right Reverend Bishop of Viviers, and to the Jesuit Fathers.

"3. I give and bequeath to the last living of the

PART TWO: *The Light*

following: Victoire Couderc, residing at La
Louvesc, Anne Buisson, also residing at La
Louvesc, Marguerite Barrial, residing at Plagnal,
and Rosalie Grégoire, residing at Aps, all that I
possess at the time of my death, of whatever it
consists or may consist in the future.

"Given and written by my hand. And I ex-
plicitly revoke all and any other preceding dispositions of my property.

"La Louvesc, September 20, 1832.

"JOHN PETER STEPHEN TERME,
"*Priest.*"

When he wrote this last will, Father Terme was
in the fullness of his youth, but he had the habit
of saying, "The really great apostles work but ten
years." And God was to take him at his word.

While he was giving a mission at Plagnal his
strength failed him. He went to his little community at Aps, his first foundation, and asked them
to receive him. Sister Agnes, formerly superior at
La Louvesc, welcomed him. But, alas, his sickness
was beyond cure. Like Saint Francis Regis, he contracted inflammation of the lungs while preaching.
Mother Thérèse was notified at once.

When they heard the sad news, the sisters of La
Louvesc recalled significant incidents that had
occurred before the Father left for the mission at
Plagnal—his last recommendations, more pressing
and more forcible than usual, the order given to
Mother Thérèse to hold two or three catechism

classes a week, his refusal to take with him all the linen prepared for his journey, and last, and above all, his farewell to the Mother Superior, when, taking the crucifix which he wore suspended about his neck, he placed it on the table and said: "Behold Him Who will be always with you." [5]

Without doubt, the Father knew he would not return.

Mother Thérèse sent a servant at once with medicines. But when he reached Plagnal, Father Terme was no more.

He died very peacefully.

To his daughters who had asked of him some final counsels, he said: "Practice unceasingly the renouncement of your own will. That is the great secret of advancement in virtue and in perfection. That does not injure the health of the body, so necessary in fulfilling the duties of our state of life. Yes, I reiterate it, practice faithfully the giving up of your own will: repeat this among yourselves. . . ." For a moment his eyes rested on a picture of the Blessed Virgin. Then his face shone with light:

"Mary, O yes, she is my Mother, and what a good Mother! In all the parishes wherein I have preached I have done all in my power to have her loved. Love her well, all of you. . . ."

When a sister voiced anxiety because the Congregation would be threatened with the loss of everything if it lost its guide, he said: "Why do you give way to such imaginations? Trust in

Divine Providence. Has Providence ever failed
you? The good God always does His work."

"My children, if you are good, God will protect
you always." Those were his last words.[6]

The servant sent by Mother Thérèse returned
on December 17th to La Louvesc, where they im-
patiently awaited him. It was seven o'clock in the
evening. He had hardly crossed the threshold of
the entrance when through all the house was heard
the cry, "Father is dead." It is impossible to describe the grief of all the sisters. Many were so
discouraged that they thought of leaving the Congregation. Mother Thérèse needed all her maternal
affection in making them realize that God would
not abandon them.

For a short time, however, everything did seem
lost. For fifteen days Mother Thérèse searched in
vain among the papers of Father Terme for evidence of his last will. If he died intestate, the
properties of the community would revert to the
family of the Founder.

Meanwhile, Father Haon, a confrère of Father
Terme, came to La Louvesc. When the Mother
Superior made her fears known to him, he said,
"But I am sure that there is a will. Tomorrow I
will offer Holy Mass in honor of Saint Philomena,
and I propose that you make a vow to place in
this chapel a tablet or a statue in her honor if the
will is found."

The next day, after Mass, Father Haon went up

to Father Terme's room. One of the first papers he came upon was the last will of Father Terme.[7] By the terms of that will, as we have seen, Mother Thérèse was made heir, together with Sisters Agnes, Stanislaus, and Joséphine.

The possession of the house at La Louvesc was assured.

IX. At School with the Society of Jesus

THE SACRIFICE which the death of Father Terme meant did not remain fruitless. Just when everything seemed endangered, the community was about to begin what were perhaps the best years it had yet known.

Indeed, the time of its well-being were the years when Mother Thérèse alone governed the community. Let us avail ourselves of the daylight: the night will come quickly enough.

As soon as the will was found, Mother Thérèse wishing to fulfill the last wish of the holy Founder, who had entrusted his daughters of the retreat to the Fathers of the Society of Jesus, wrote to Father Renault, the Provincial of France.[1] Father Renault was not a stranger to her. Once traveling through

La Louvesc he had visited the House of Saint Regis and had had a long conversation with the superior.

The following are some extracts from the letter of Mother Thérèse under date of December, 1834:

"MY VERY REVEREND FATHER:

"The interest you showed in our little Congregation when you did us the honor of visiting us, greatly encourages me to come to you now, and in the extremity of need in which we find ourselves to seek from you some help in our misfortune.

"We have just lost our Father, the worthy superior whom the Lord was pleased to give us. We are alone: without protector, without guide. What will become of us, or, rather, what will become of this work of God? For us ourselves, wholly submissive to the will of Divine Providence, we adore His decrees. If He send us opprobrium and contempt, far from murmuring, our afflicted hearts are resigned, and whatever be in store for us, I venture to hope that we will not cease to bless the Hand that strikes us. But we cannot be indifferent to the work of Our Lord.

"The sad condition to which we now see it reduced overwhelms us. Must it be given up, or may we hope, my Very Reverend Father, that you will come to our aid? It is in the name of God's own glory, for the salvation of souls, that I come to beg your good-will. I know these are very strong reasons why we may plead with you in favor of the Congregation of Saint Regis.

"We are as yet in the cradle. It will be necessary therefore to have a Father who will train us, a guide who will lead us. You alone can give us such a one. Will our expectations be in vain? We plead with you not to abandon the poor afflicted ones.

"Only a Jesuit Father can continue, can make firm the work with which Saint Regis, for his glory, knew how to inspire the heart of this worthy priest who for so many reasons merits our keen sorrow."

The Reverend Father Renault could not turn a deaf ear to such an urgent appeal. His answer to Mother Thérèse is the following letter:

"Metz, January 12, 1835.

"I already knew, Reverend and good Mother, the sad news of which your letter tells, and which is the reason for your tears. When I first heard it, my immediate thought was of you, poor Mother. My heart went out to you. I learned to appreciate the qualities of mind and of heart of this excellent Father. Indeed, I would have received him into the Society had I not felt how necessary his presence still was to your Community. So I postponed his coming to a future date. If I had received him, he would not have been able to give you all the service which he did give.

"We will do for you, my good Mother, all that he himself would do for you were he still with us,

and we will do it always. We will do more. While
we are waiting until the Bishop finds one who is
fitted for the work, I will, for the time being, dispense your Community from certain rules; but
there are rules that must not be touched. That is
as far as we can go, and almost regretting that we
cannot go further, we nevertheless offer you our
guidance, our consolations and our prayers.

"You may go with full confidence to the Fathers
at La Louvesc. They will be happy to serve you in
every way they can.

"I am in the union of prayer and of sorrow also,
Reverend and very dear Mother, your most humble and devoted servant in Our Lord,

"FRANCIS RENAULT, S.J."

This letter of Father Renault was a veritable ray
of sunlight in a sky of darkness.

Just at that time Bishop Bonnel notified Mother
Thérèse that he had appointed Father Béchetoille
of Annonay superior of the community. "I have
selected him," said the Bishop, "because of all the
priests of my diocese, I know of none better fitted
to take the place of Father Terme, nor anyone else
who could be more helpful to you both in things
temporal and things spiritual."

When this letter came, Mother Thérèse called
the sisters together and sought their counsel. All
were of one mind—that she should go to Viviers
and beseech the Bishop not to give them a secular
priest as their superior.

The next day, Mother Thérèse set out with Sister Joséphine and Mlle. de Bronac. The Bishop received them warmly and with all good-will. Sister Joséphine records that he said: "You speak, not to a Bishop, but to a kind and loving father."

"During the first part of our interview we could not restrain our tears. The Bishop also lamented the holy priest who had labored so zealously in his diocese. He deigned to say: 'I take you under my protection. I have named Father Béchetoille your superior because I believe he can be helpful to you.' We thanked him very much, but we asked him to be good enough to allow us to put before him the condition of our Congregation with its spiritual and temporal needs. He freely gave the permission, saying in a kindly manner: 'Confide in me in every way.' Mother Thérèse then spoke to him of the necessity of help from the Jesuit Fathers, both for the training of the members of the Congregation themselves, and for the Exercises of the general retreats. She set forth the mind of the entire community on this point.

"The Bishop understood our reasons and promised us to write himself to Father Renault, asking him to take us under his care."

The sisters, of course, were well satisfied.

By an unfortunate coincidence, while Mother Thérèse pleaded with the Bishop for the appointment of a Jesuit as their superior, Father Béchetoille having received the notification of his appointment, presented himself as superior at the

House of Saint Regis. For a moment embarrass-
ment reigned: but the sisters' fears were quickly
dissipated. Sister Victorine frankly told him just
what the business was that had taken Mother
Thérèse to Viviers. Father Béchetoille was humble
enough not to stand on formalities. When later the
Bishop recalled his appointment, he said: "The
action is just; one cannot cultivate a field he does
not know." [2]

The way to the realization of the hopes of Father
Terme was therefore open. The Society of Jesus—
just as he had requested—was to take charge of the
little infant Congregation. To the Society, the
Cenacle would eventually owe its rules and a
great many of its customs. For many years to come
the successive provincials at Lyons, and the superiors at La Louvesc, would strive to give to the
Sisters of Saint Regis, or, as we will very soon call
them, the Religious of the Cenacle, the purest
spirit of the Spiritual Exercises.

So, much of the light that enlightened them will
come from those to whom Father Terme had confided them.

The sky will not always be cloudless. God will
permit that some of the decisive rulings given by
the Fathers of the Society shall be for the Sisters
veritable crucifixions. We will speak both of the
darkness and of the light. Both the night and the
day yield glory to the Lord.

*　　*　　*

Father Renault, informed of the Bishop's wishes, went to La Louvesc to assume charge of the little unshepherded flock. He began by interrogating each sister in private. Manifestly the Father Provincial was determined to clear up an initial doubt, for every sister heard him ask this question: "Are you satisfied with conducting retreats or do you wish to teach a class of children?" "The work of retreats will be our chief work," was the answer given to Father Renault, "for Father Terme some time before his death made known to us that he wished that his daughters should engage only in the giving of retreats."

"Since that is so," Father Renault replied, "I promise to aid you by every means in my power."

And then he made known to the sisters a fact which the Congregation has never forgotten.

"As I thoughtfully considered the last will of Father Terme, not knowing whether I should interest myself in you or not, I thought I heard a voice saying to me: 'Take care of this infant lying upon the straw.'

"At the same time I felt an interior urge to give to this very young work my care and my devoted service." [3]

These words comforted the sisters very much. As for Father Renault, he never forgot the voice he had heard, and either in person or through some subordinate he directed the formative years of the daughters of the retreat.

The first of the Fathers directed to carry on this

apostolate was Father Sellier. (Father Valentin was the superior at La Louvesc.)

"I requested him," wrote Father Renault, "to draw up your rules, since he already knew your house." Having lived at La Louvesc ever since 1832, in which year the Society had accepted on the invitation of Father Terme the care of the pilgrimage, he had frequent occasion to see the Sisters of Saint Regis at close range. He gave himself at once to the work, but was soon obliged to abandon his task, feeling that he was incapable of writing rules for a congregation the purpose of which though one in theory was manysided in practice. Mother Thérèse has recorded in a letter her gratitude to Father Sellier, who wished to give them the light that would lead them. "I trust he will be permitted to serve us as much by his prayers as he willed to serve us by his labors."

Meanwhile another superior was appointed to La Louvesc. Father Rigaud succeeded Father Valentin. To Father Rigaud the Cenacle owes much. So far as the Exercises are concerned it is no exaggeration to say that he gave to those at the House of Saint Regis the first training therein that they had received since the death of Father Terme. Nevertheless the training was hard on both sides. Father Rigaud appeared distant, reserved, in striking contrast to the fatherly ways of good Father Valentin, who had been universally regretted. Two months were required for establishing mutual confidence, but once the ice was broken, Father Rigaud was understood and loved as a father. Backed by the authorizations which the Father Provincial had given him, he filled the rôle of a true master of novices, spending a great part of his days in moulding these sisters into religious. For up to that time, it must be admitted, they had had no unity of direction. The archives of the house at La Louvesc hold the records of this labor, very detailed and almost continuous, of the superior of the Jesuits.

The first act of Father Rigaud was to separate the novitiate from the community. The novices then had their own special spiritual exercises. There were two conferences a day, one in the morning, the other in the afternoon, given either by Sister Victorine, who was all this while mistress of novices, or by Father Rigaud himself. The latter was kind enough to instruct the sisters in the recitation of the Office of the Blessed Virgin, which the Father Provincial had ordered the community to recite.[4]

But the principal work of this wise director was to give the religious an understanding of the Exercises of Saint Ignatius. To this end, he directed the sisters to give one half hour every day to the study of the book of the Exercises, with the obligation of noting down every one of their difficulties, so that they might have them explained later.[5] Because of this practice, Mother Thérèse and the other sisters had in the end a full understanding of the true meaning of the book of Saint Ignatius.

PART TWO: *The Light*

About this time, under the superiorship of Father Rigaud, a Jesuit Father sent by the Father Provincial came to the House of Saint Regis. Since eventually he will play an important part in the history of the Cenacle, we should note his first visit to La Louvesc: that visit marked a conference to the sisters which had far-reaching consequences.

Father Fouillot was at that time instructor of the Fathers making their tertianship at Saint Acheul. When Father Sellier had declined the task of drawing up the Rule, the Father Provincial sought one who would do this. He thought of Father Fouillot and asked him to make the journey to La Louvesc and study at first hand the Saint Regis House.

Father Fouillot accordingly went, and spoke to the entire community.

It is interesting to read the record which Mother Thérèse made of this first visit.

"We realized from the moment of his arrival among us, how much Father Fouillot esteemed our work. The good Father asked us time and again to pray for him, since he thought the task of writing the Rule a very difficult one. 'I need,' he said, 'help from on high: and through your prayers I hope to secure it.' But he also desired every one of us to tell him what she thought of the Congregation: of the manner in which it should be organized. Finally he said, 'Since you have conducted retreats, put in writing for me all the pertinent questions you can think of.' " [6]

One feels that in this paragraph Mother Thérèse gives the kernel of the conference which Father Fouillot delivered to the sisters of the Saint Regis House. . . . After he had begged prayers for the work he had in hand, the Father added something wholly unexpected: "You are as yet small in number; you will grow more numerous with time. Courage and confidence; it will be so. Apropos of this, I know well one who is far away from here. Oh! if you could realize what a beautiful soul she is. She has an immense fortune, but beyond this, her virtues are admirable. Indeed, my sisters, her virtue exceeds her fortune by as much as her fortune exceeds yours." [7]

This good soul of whom Father Fouillot spoke came through him to know the sisters of La Louvesc. Owing to the favorable recommendations given by him to Father Renault, she eventually supplanted Mother Thérèse, who was put to one side.

The visit of Father Fouillot was like the prelude to a painful drama. Mother Thérèse would have been astonished if anyone had then said to her, "This widow of such admirable virtue, whose name you have just heard, will be for you the cause of great suffering."

* * *

To the names of Father Rigaud and Father Fouillot must be added that of Father Augry, a humble worker whose task it was to teach the daughters of Father Terme how to conduct retreats. He never had charge of the community, as Father Rigaud had, but in his free time he came to explain, either in common or individually to the community, the way of retreats according to the book of Saint Ignatius. He commented on the Directory, then, one after another, the annotations, the additions, and even the rules for the discerning of spirits.[8]

This hidden work won him no great notice but the Cenacle owes much to him as commentator on the Exercises, and Mother Thérèse was oftentimes the docile pupil in his classes.

These are the three great masters that God gave to the Religious of the Cenacle. Father Rigaud moulded the interior life, Father Fouillot labored to compile the Rule of the community, Father Augry taught them the very difficult art of giving the Spiritual Exercises.

Needless to say, the general direction of Father Renault guided the particular work of the others. As long as he was provincial he gave his care "to the infant placed upon the straw." If later he withdrew, it was never in any final way. We will see him reappear at a critical hour, at the call of Mother Thérèse; we will learn also that some years before his death he received from the Father Provincial at Paris the commission—one very pleasing to his heart—of moulding the young novices of the Cenacle.

For such great care given by the Society of

Jesus in making the daughters of Father Terme religious after God's own Heart, they have ever and in all places given the evidence of most touching gratitude. The words of Mother de Larochenégly, Superior General of the Cenacle, express that gratitude most truly: "The Society of Jesus will always be our mother; and we will remain bound to it as the branch of the vine is bound to its stem." [9]

X. The Two Branches

O N A DAY of the summer of 1835 a carriage made its upward way to La Louvesc. Within it was a woman, in heavy mourning. She was but eighteen years of age. Her name was Élisa Gallet. She was the widow of M. Gallet, a notary of La Tour du Pin. Their happiness was of short duration. A short while after their marriage M. Gallet became dangerously ill. Every human help proved ineffective. The wife made a vow that she would go on pilgrimage to the tomb of Saint Francis Regis if her husband recovered or, since he was not a practical Catholic, if he should return to the Faith before he died. This latter grace she obtained for him. On the day of which we speak she had come to thank the Saint.

PART TWO: *The Light*

Looking out of the carriage, she saw the house of the sisters. "What institution is that?" she asked the driver. "That," he answered, "is the house of the Religious of Saint Regis."

During her stay at La Louvesc, Mme. Gallet for the guidance of her conscience consulted one of the Fathers of the priests' house—Father Garnier. He, without any ulterior motive, advised her to visit Mother Thérèse. Mme. Gallet did so, and almost as soon as she saw the Mother, she felt impelled to open her soul to her: "There is no obstacle to my becoming a religious. The infant daughter whom God gave me is dead. I will enter as soon as you will sanction it."

Mother Thérèse led her through the house. Entering the room wherein the Exercises were taught, Mme. Gallet was much impressed by the picture of Saint Philomena, the votive offering placed there because of the finding of Father Terme's will. "What is that picture?" Mme. Gallet asked. Mother Thérèse explained to her why it had been placed there. "But it has no frame," Mme Gallet said. "I will take pleasure in sending you one." The frame was not long in coming, and a short while afterwards—in June, 1835—Mme. Gallet entered as a novice.[1]

She was to give something besides a frame to the Religious of the Cenacle. She was to give the example of a life filled with the love of God, and of the sweetest death imaginable. This young widow of twenty lived only two years in religion, and she

[71]

was the first daughter of Mother Thérèse to receive her heavenly reward. A few pages further on, we will read of her last hours.

For the moment, let us re-live that novitiate so full of fervor, into which she had just entered.

More than one characteristic reveals to us the deep, supernatural spirit of these young souls. But we cite only one. To some it will seem naïve, to many others it will appear exaggerated; but there is no proof that God shared either of these opinions.

"Our poverty," we read in a contemporary record, "was so extreme, that it could go no further. The young sister who was time-keeper, and who we may be sure had no watch, rose at a guess as to the time, and having neither matches nor candle, groped her way to the clock to find the hour by touching its hands. When the novice acquainted Mother Thérèse with her manner of arousing the community, the latter said to her: 'This little difficulty ought not to discourage you, my Sister. God will come to our aid. Poverty will be our greatest safeguard.' " [2]

If all the novices had as great longing for perfection as this young time-keeper, one understands the comment of Mother Thérèse on this period of the community life. "Conditions could hardly have been better; union of hearts, peace, charity, reigned to such an extent that I still dwell with happiness upon what I felt then in being part of that little community." [3]

Part Two: *The Light*

In the meanwhile, the agonizing question which had presented itself to Father Terme still faced the superiors. No solution had as yet been found. Should the Sisters of Saint Regis undertake the two works—the giving of retreats, and teaching in the schools? The Jesuit Fathers, consulted on the matter, were of the mind that both works should not be undertaken. Consequently Father Renault decided that on the occasion of the next general retreat every subject should be questioned as to her tastes, and examined most carefully as to her abilities.

That inquiry gave the following result: fifteen religious were judged fitted to give retreats; twenty should keep on with their teaching. It remained only to fix the date of separation.

Father Rigaud went down to Viviers to confer with the diocesan authority. Bishop Bonnel approved everything and fixed June 16th, the Feast of Saint Regis, as the date on which the fifteen sisters selected for the retreat work should change their habit. Those who were to devote themselves to teaching would keep the old habit and return to the schools. No difficulty seemed likely to present itself until Sisters Agnes and Stanislaus declared to Mother Thérèse, who had advised them of the decision made by the Bishop and by the Father Provincial of the Society, that they were to be assigned to the retreat work: "We will never give up teaching, for that is the true work of the Founder."

A Great and Humble Soul

Their choice was respected. Sister Agnes, who, it will be remembered, had been the first superior at La Louvesc, and Sister Stanislaus (Nanette Buisson) who, as we have seen, was so devoted to Father Terme during the building of the house, returned to the schools.[4]

It would have been wiser, perhaps, when there was a question of choosing between the two branches, not to have asserted so emphatically that only one of the two works was the true work of Father Terme. That statement ran the risk of giving offence and causing consequent suffering on both sides. More than one trouble would have been avoided if when separating each one had considered only the divine call which she heard—whether it was to the work of retreats or to that of teaching. At least no insidious comparisons should ever have been made publicly.

Yet who would presume to blame these religious, made sensitive by a thousand little things which always under like circumstances assume great proportions? They so deeply loved the Saint Regis House that the separation caused their hearts to suffer.

Supernatural souls quickly meet again in harmony. The proof that they who went away sought harmony is that they asked Mother Thérèse to continue to direct them.

She was wise enough not to accept the invitation, but she was nevertheless touched by this parting evidence of the veneration which her children of

yesterday had given to her. Profound assuredly
was her joy when Sister Agnes and Sister Stanislaus
came three years after the separation to make their
retreat at the Saint Regis House.

Again, the material difficulties resulting from
this unexpected circumstance in the separation
were great. Of Father Terme's four heirs, two
stayed with the retreat work; two went to the
schools. As soon as the incident was known by him,
the Bishop asked about the division of the property. The best way, it seemed, was to divide the
property equally between the Sisters of the Retreat and the Teaching Sisters. As a result, the
Teaching Sisters kept all the schools, the Religious
of the Retreat, the house at La Louvesc.[5]

Thus was the separation which God's merciful
plan had permitted brought to a successful issue.[6]

Two separate families would henceforth venerate Father Terme. The Sisters of Saint Regis
were to make their name blessed among the Chris-
tian people of Ardèche and of Lozère. The Religious of the Retreat were to spread and prosper
to an extent that only the sacrifice of a chosen soul
could explain, for Mother Thérèse's hour had
come, the hour for which God had sent her, the
hour of the cross.

After ten years in the light, she is to enter into
the shadow, by half a century of humiliations, to
obtain from God the fruition of that grain sown in
His field. All of which proves that one may be
foundress in the eyes of God, and in the eyes of

men be a person of no account. It would not surprise us if this were the lesson which Providence wished Mother Thérèse Couderc to teach us.

The brethren of Jesus said to Him: "Manifest Thyself to the world." Jesus answered: "My time is not yet come." That meant that Jesus Christ was not to manifest Himself truly save on the Cross. Jesus saved the world, Jesus has made the sowing-time of all sowers fruitful not by working wonders, not even by praying, but by dying. "And I, if I be lifted up from the earth, will draw all things to Myself." "The disciple is not above his Master."

It was by dying every day—every day of more than forty years—that Mother Thérèse sanctified the Cenacle, and made it fruitful.

XI. The Storm

AS A PREPARATION for Calvary, God granted His servant the favor of the perpetual vows. She pronounced them January 6, 1837. On that Feast of the Epiphany her heart offered to God the gold of her charity, the incense of a life henceforth wholly hidden in prayer. And had she known what the future held for her, her generosity would have placed at the feet of the Divine Infant, with still greater love, the bitter myrrh of her trials. They began on April 14th.

PART TWO: *The Light*

On that day Mother Thérèse went to her bed, not to rise from it until June 24th. God thus sent His servant into retreat the better to prepare her for the cross.

Towards the end of May, that cross threw its first shadow.

The reader will remember the young widow who, seeing the St. Regis House on her journey, felt called upon to consecrate herself to God forever within its walls. Madame Gallet was one of the well-beloved children of the Foundress, and now, on May 22nd, they were obliged to administer Extreme Unction. From her own bed Mother Thérèse followed every phase of the painful sickness. Both the mother and the daughter, lost in abandonment to the Divine Will, suffered, separated one from the other, but their hearts were as one.

On May 25th Mother Thérèse granted permission to Sister Gallet to take the vows. Soon after, the last agony of the young professed began. Such illumination came to her by an act of faith as is met with only among the greatest servants of God.

The young widow of twenty longed for heaven, but it seemed to her that she had no right to go there without the permission of her superior. So she repeated ceaselessly these three words: "No, not yet." As the sisters who cared for her did not grasp the meaning of the words, they went to consult Mother Thérèse about them, who immediately said: "Tell her I give her permission to die."

Receiving this answer from the Mother she

loved so well, the gentle soul in her agony murmured: "Oh, how I thank you." It was as if she only waited for that word in order to depart: "Jesus, Mary, Joseph," she said, and then expired.[1] Mother Thérèse was not even permitted to look upon her for the last time.

However, by the end of June the venerated invalid could be lifted from her bed, and little by little her strength returned. But rest was still imperative. So the Father Superior at La Louvesc advised her to go down to Notre-Dame d'Ay.

She remained there until September 14th, served with affection by good Sister Julie, the infirmarian, one of the first sisters of the Congregation.

At Notre-Dame d'Ay, August 15th and September 8th are days of reverent celebration. Did Mother Thérèse wish to express her gratitude to the Blessed Virgin for health restored? Did she desire, now that the separation had been effected, to offer to Mary in a special way those whom Father Terme called the Daughters of the Retreat? The day of the Assumption was ever a day on which, surrounded by some of her sisters who came to celebrate the feast with her—for they came thus without fail to their venerated Mother—she would solemnly consecrate all her daughters to the Blessed Virgin. Indeed, she did more than this.

Under the inspiration of God she surrendered her superiorship into the hands of Mary, declaring that she would henceforth give no order, nor come to any decision without having first invoked her authorization. Following is her resolution, dictated, surely, by the Holy Spirit:

"O glorious Virgin Mary, Mother of my God, Queen of heaven and of earth, my protectress, my advocate and my Mother, deign to look with kindness and mercy on the most unworthy of thy daughters and to accept the offering I make of myself and of all that belongs to me.

"To thee I consecrate my body, my soul, my mind, my heart. I wish henceforth to be wholly occupied in loving thee and in making thee loved. Innumerable times have I consecrated myself to thee. Innumerable times has it been necessary to renew that consecration. Pardon, I beg of thee, my good and tender Mother, pardon my inconstancy, my vacillation. Grant that I may never forget thee again. I intend on the contrary that from this day, August 15, 1837, they may be able to say that my love for thee has gone on increasing. And, my good Mother, I consecrate to thee not only all that belongs to me personally, I consecrate to thee, and pray thee to receive among thy daughters, my dear sisters whom I love and for whom I desire perfection as for myself. Deign to take them all under thy protection, remembering, O my august princess, that this little community and all the daughters who compose it have been already consecrated to thee by thy faithful servant, our good Father Terme.

"I pray thee also, my blessed Mother, to aid all the souls who follow the exercises of the retreat in your house. I say 'your' house because I no longer look upon it as belonging to anyone but thee. Indeed, today I lay down my superiority. Whenever it is necessary to discharge any of the functions incumbent on my office, I will first ask permission of thee, having no right to act of myself, since I have given all to thee.

"In concluding this consecration, O my beloved Mother, I implore thee to obtain for me the grace to act always from supernatural motives, that self may be as if it did not exist. Amen; amen; amen."

The oblation was complete. Mary accepted it.

* * *

We must go back some months to understand well what we are about to relate.

Madame Gallet was absolute mistress of her fortune. When she entered the novitiate she made a gift of all she possessed to Mother Thérèse, who, with the authorization of Mme. Gallet and that of Father Renault, decided to build a chapel at once and to make an addition to the house, now altogether too small. No difficulty was experienced during the lifetime of Mme. Gallet. The chapel, at her death, was all but completed, the other building plans quite far advanced, when suddenly a rumor, more and more persistent, led to the belief that the family of Mme. Gallet would contest the will. If the rumor were well founded, great financial difficulties would result.

One day while Mother Thérèse prayed at Notre-Dame d'Ay—it was shortly after her act of consecration—she was seized with sudden fright concerning the future material well-being of the Congregation.

"One would say," she related later, "that the scales fell from my eyes. I asked myself why I had built the chapel, added to the present building, for I saw clearly that on the one hand the hard climate would make increase of novices most difficult, and on the other, that the Society would be crippled by debt."

On her return to La Louvesc on September 14th, she told her fears to several of the sisters, among others a novice who had some months before been appointed procurator of the house. This novice, frightened perhaps by the anxieties which harassed the superior, drew up for Father Renault, then at La Louvesc, a balance sheet showing all the debts which Mother Thérèse had contracted. According to her report, they amounted to thirty-seven thousand francs—an erroneous total, for in it was included a gift made by Mme. Gallet during the latter's lifetime, to which her family had no possible title. The entire debts contracted by Mother Thérèse did not really exceed ten thousand francs.

Father Renault, usually so wise and so deliberate, permitted the report to upset him, and—it is almost unbelievable when one remembers the sensitiveness of his own heart—he presented to the venerated Mother on October 15th, her feast day, as he extended his good wishes in the presence of the entire community, a paper on which was written the indebtedness to the amount of thirty-seven thousand francs, saying to her at the same time: "Here, Mother, is a bouquet for your feast day."

The poor Mother could not restrain her tears. She could scarcely see. Several of her daughters felt constrained to encourage her, telling her that all that had been undertaken was necessary, and that the good God would provide therefor.[2]

These first tears of Mother Thérèse were to be followed by many others.

The report of the procurator had deeply impressed Father Renault. Fearing that the generosity of Mother Thérèse would endanger the financial condition of the house, he determined to vest authority henceforth in a council composed of the superior, the procurator and three other sisters.

Observing the safeguards set by the Father Provincial for the right working of this new body, one is obliged to admit that his confidence in the humble Mother was not what it had been.

This new order was established on October 21st. The following day the first meeting was held. Mother Thérèse found herself in the minority.

Alas! once authority was taken from her hands,

fervor vanished as if by magic. Under the superiorship of Mother Thérèse silence was so well observed that visiting strangers asked if anybody
lived in the Saint Regis House. "One wouldn't
recognize the community today," wrote Mother
Joséphine. "Silence no longer reigns: recollection
is no longer practised."

Amid these trials the year 1837 ended. The year
1838 was to mark the true Calvary. By the more
and more mysterious providence of God, after the
mistake of Father Renault with regard to the de-
pendability of the novice charged with the office
of procurator, Father Fouillot, in his turn, was to
make the mistake of sending to La Louvesc that
very rich and, as he thought, virtuous woman, of
whom he had spoken on the occasion of his first
visit to the sisters.

Madame de La Villeurnoy was, alas! the lamentable new year's gift to the Sisters of Saint
Regis. The day she crossed the threshold of the
house, she brought the cross to Mother Thérèse.

This cross did not reveal itself at once. On the
contrary, the community shared the opinion of
Father Fouillot. Nor were they surprised to learn
that Father Renault had decided to make an exception in Mme. de La Villeurnoy's case and give
her the habit after only fifteen days' postulancy.[3]

We do not know if Mother Thérèse understood
the real reason for such a step. It would be surprising, however, if she did not, for supernatural
light searches out the deepest obscurities.

However that may be, further doubt was impossible. Father Renault had made up his mind that this widow should replace Mother Thérèse. His reasoning may easily be reconstructed, and it would be unfair not to do this. Two dangers threatened the community—those of which Mother Thérèse had caught a glimpse in the chapel of Notre-Dame d'Ay: lack of subjects; lack of money. Madame de La Villeurnoy, because of her name and her family's distinction, would draw postulants; while by reason of her fortune, she would be able to pay the debts. Father Fouillot stood ready to answer for her virtue. Why not, then, charge her with the office of superior? Such a step seemed to assure the future of the little Society.

A hundred years away, and knowing that the plan was a complete failure, it is easy for us to criticize Father Renault. At that time he acted in accordance with what he believed to be for the greatest good of all. The Religious of the Cenacle, worthy daughters of their Mother, have always so judged his act, and in spite of the trials which, wholly involuntarily, Father Renault brought upon Mother Thérèse, they always cherish for him sentiments of the most filial affection and of the most profound veneration.

Madame de La Villeurnoy was in the novitiate only a few days when Father Renault asked her to come down to Viviers. He wished to present her to the Bishop and to have her named Superior General in place of Mother Thérèse. He had, some time before, asked Mother Thérèse to surrender her charge.

Bishop Bonnel approved the plan of Father Renault, and the novice of a few days went back to La Louvesc, Superior General.

The episcopal notification of the deposition of Mother Thérèse was given: Father Renault presented their new Mother to the daughters of Saint Regis—and all was officially consummated.

God alone knows what Mother Thérèse suffered in this painful situation. "And do you think," she said one day to a religious who had suffered humiliation, "that I did not suffer in being set aside!"

We believe, however, that we do not deceive ourselves in saying that her greatest agony sprang from the fear of those trials which she foresaw would fall upon her well-beloved daughters. Her Mother's heart had wished that they might be spared such a Calvary.

Following is the text of the documents dealing with her deposition. To appreciate the virtue of Mother Thérèse we must picture her as just one of the number of the Religious of Saint Regis, listening to the reading of these sentences, more than one of which expressed in ill-disguised terms censure of her administration.

A Great and Humble Soul
The Letter of Bishop Bonnel

Viviers, October 23, 1838.

MY MOST BELOVED DAUGHTERS:

The interest which I feel in your infant Congregation of Saint Regis, the principal work of which is the giving of retreats to women eager to make certain their eternal salvation, has led me to consider the means that will consolidate your work and put it in the way of securing that perfection of which it is capable. The result of our study has been that the spiritual and temporal welfare of your infant Community demands that Mme. de La Villeurnoy be appointed Superior Foundress, that Mlle. Couderc, otherwise Sister Thérèse, be Assistant, and Mlle. Chareyre, or Sister Augustine, be Mistress of Novices. The Sister to be procurator will be named later. This arrangement has seemed to me the more proper since I have been assured that all the members of the Community take the same view. I ask God that the most perfect union reign among you, and that no spirit of insubordination will ever show itself. Such is the very sincere wish of my heart. I give unto all my fatherly blessing.

✠FRANÇOIS,
Bishop of Viviers.

We call attention in passing to the use by the Bishop of Viviers of the title: *"Superior Found-*

ress." Mother Thérèse must, then, give up not
only her title as superior, but also surrender to
this novice, who had passed but a few days in the
community, the glory which would be hers as the
one who founded the Congregation.

The letter of Father Renault is much longer,
but it is equally severe for the heart of the poor
Mother. It shows, it is true, what does not surprise
us, that Mother Thérèse had asked, as would all
superiors who act after God's own Heart, to be re-
lieved of her burden. One finds in this letter not
a word of thanks to Mother Thérèse, but, on the
contrary,—just as in the Bishop's letter—the con-
ferring of the title of "Foundress" on Mme. de La
Villeurnoy, the declaration that she is the savior
sent by God; and finally, that the poor victim may
in no way be spared, it is ordered that she herself
read this letter to her former daughters.

Avignon, October 29, 1838.

MY DEAR MOTHER:

It was not my wish to write to you. I would have
preferred, convinced as I am that your own fidelity
and your own heart are sufficient inspiration for
you, to leave you to yourself, with no intermediary
between your former daughters and their new
Mother, all the more as you yourself, more than
once, have asked to be freed from the burden.
Moreover, when I told you of the arrival of Mme.
de La Villeurnoy you answered me by saying that

your happiness would be complete if you had nothing else to do but to obey her as your good and worthy Mother. Yes, I am convinced that in all this you have not gone against yourself in any way.

It is certain that those at Viviers have sought only the greatest good of the Congregation, without—just as should be the case—the slightest distinction of persons. As for myself, I confined myself to laying open the real state of things—the reasons for, and the reasons against, whatever they were—leaving it to the Bishop and his Vicars General to think over these conditions.

All have unanimously decided that Mme. de La Villeurnoy, whom Providence has sent to you, being already by the force of circumstances Superior in fact, should be such by title also: and should be considered, in order that false attitudes may be avoided, as Superior Foundress of this little infant Congregation. Consider what its situation was last year, and what it is today. Let us thank God Who, without doubt, has done everything; but let us not forget the instrument by whom He has served Himself and who will, I hope, continue to be the channel of His favors; because to forget her will be to underestimate the action of Divine Providence, and our obligations to her.

You have, therefore, my good Mother, received that which you asked, and Mme. de La Villeurnoy, that which she most certainly never sought. I have admired, I assure you, her silent devotion and sacrifice. She has uttered no word: she has permitted the burden to be laid upon her. She is not ignorant, however, of all that she will have to suffer, both from within and from without, above all in the beginning when there will be so much and so many things to do.

But I have told her that amid all her sufferings and her cares she may ever count on the good-will of all her daughters. I have, indeed, assured her that all of you will work with her as with one heart and one soul. I have told her that you, my dear daughter, will be the guarantee of this perfect union, and if by any possibility one among you should not show towards her perfect submission of heart, as she ought, that I am certain you will use all your dominating influence to lead back such a one to sentiments more conformable to the vow and spirit of obedience; that you will see in the office of Assistant only the means of aiding more effectively this good Mother, of entering into her thoughts, of making the authority, with which God for your good has invested her, loved.

It is impossible, then, for you not to be closely united in the one same spirit with your Superior. To think the contrary would be but to do injustice to you. But so great is my desire for this perfect union, that I ask you (I myself rather hesitate to do so) to tell your former daughters the promises I have made in their name. Make these known to the Sisters, whose edifying spirit pleases me, to the Mothers who should outstrip the Sisters in all that is edifying, since they are the better informed and should give the better example.

Read this letter to them and let me know in your answer to me whether or not I have deceived myself.

No, I am very certain I have not deceived myself. All of you will prove yourselves worthy of your calling by showing yourselves, through a supernatural submission to your Superior and a perfect union of heart with her, worthy daughters of this good Mother whom God has sent to you from afar to aid you in your distress, and who has shown herself so good, so generous, so devoted towards you, and whom your Bishop has given to you. In so acting, you, my dear daughters, will win higher titles in my esteem, in my respect, and in the affection that I bear for you in Our Lord.

With ever the same feelings towards you, my good Mother, I am your most humble and devoted servant in Jesus Christ,

FRANCIS RENAULT, S.J.

There remains but the reading of the admirable letter of Mother Thérèse, written from her heart. It is so beautiful, so thoroughly supernatural, so profoundly humble, that reading it one is filled with reverence and would feign lift it to his lips as he would the reliquary of a saint—a martyr.

"MY WELL-BELOVED ONES:

"Divine Providence, Who has ever so opportunely cared for the needs of the Sisters of Saint Regis, gives us now fresh evidence of His paternal care in sending us, sending both to you and to me, a Mother entitled to our full esteem and our full confidence, in the person of Mme. de La Villeurnoy.

"I am very much pleased, my dear Sisters, to announce with my own lips her nomination by the Bishop, who has approved it. I confidently trust that you will hear this announcement with pleasure and that from this day forth you will look upon Mme. de La Villeurnoy as your good Mother. You already know the interest and affection with which she has been good enough to honor us. It is for us to strive, my very dear Sisters, to give answer by our best, to lighten for her, if it be possible, the burden of her office as Superior; to lighten it by our obedience, our respect, our zeal —above all else, by our religious perfection. It is time indeed to labor that we may become true religious. I know, my dear Sisters, your desires and good-will, and I count upon your worthiest disposition of mind and heart.

"Pray for me: I will pray for you. I am with sincere attachment,

"Your very humble,
"MARIE-THÉRÈSE."

O beata humilitas!

A Great and Humble Soul

*   *   *

And now the shadows lengthen. For nearly forty-five years the light will be veiled. Only at the very last hour of day will the darkness, suddenly breaking, reveal a magnificent sunset.

The Shadow

XII. Silence and Fortitude

O N OCTOBER 23, 1838, Mme. de La Villeurnoy was named by the Bishop of Viviers "Superior Foundress" of the Sisters of Saint Regis.
Eleven months later, September 24, 1839, the same
Bishop of Viviers deposed her. Of her rule, so short
and yet altogether too long, there has remained the
memory of great sufferings endured by the community—"so great," Mother Thérèse wrote one
day, "that the Sisters could not have endured the
trial any longer."

The most truthful and the kindest thing that
one can say of Mme. de La Villeurnoy is, that she
had not the slightest notion of the religious life,
still less was she one capable of living up to the
title of Foundress given her by the Bishop and by
Father Renault.

Her first care seemed to be to drive out of the
Saint Regis House that outstanding poverty which
Mother Thérèse had always maintained therein.

So, having to return to Paris on family business,
in December, 1838, some weeks after her election,
she sent therefrom many things destined to make
life easier for the religious. About the same time,

furniture, rugs, plates and dishes, bedding, came from her Château de Soupirs to La Louvesc, and to Tournon, a residence purchased by Mother Thérèse for the sick Sisters, and for the Mothers through the more rigorous winters. Madame de La Villeurnoy hastened to furnish the latter, her intention being to bring the entire community there for the winter of 1839, which eventually came to pass.[1]

Of all the bounties of the Viscountess, there only remain at La Louvesc two chandeliers, still hanging in the chapel, silent witnesses to those days of ill omen when as the house was completed there fell, stone by stone, the wall of that poverty without which no religious life can ever be preserved.

Indeed, in a short while the greatest confusion reigned.

At and around La Louvesc the changed circumstances of the Saint Regis House were looked upon as very strange, and within the community itself uneasiness reigned between subjects and superior.

Dissatisfaction and confusion are the distinctive marks of the mental atmosphere emanating from the rule of this newly elected one. We should also make mention of the disorderly state of the finances. When she was deposed, the debts aggregated about one hundred and twenty-eight thousand francs, and later Mother de Larochenégly, then Superior General of the Congregation, wrote that fifteen years would be required to undo the evil wrought by this deplorable administration of eleven months.

But out of evil God brings good. In His Hands Mme. de La Villeurnoy was a marvelous instrument for the sanctification of Mother Thérèse. The latter showed herself wholly admirable. The situation was extremely delicate, the more so since the community realized that Mme. de La Villeurnoy would set them all adrift. Virtue less enlightened or less solid than that of Mother Thérèse could easily have led her to profit by the circumstances—to take the helm again or at least to win for herself sympathy and votes. But there was nothing like that. Deposed, she accepted her deposition in the fullest sense of the word. She looked upon Mme. de La Villeurnoy as the representative of God, permitting herself no criticism nor even giving herself to confidences.

In silence and in the hope of better days, according to the words of Holy Scripture, she found her strength: *In silentio et spe erit fortitudo mea.*

In regard to this, the sole incident which comes to us from her during these eleven months of Calvary is significant. Such external evidences are rare enough in the life of Mother Thérèse, since God wished to make of her the great silent one, the great unknown. Over such of these as God has permitted to be handed down to us, let us ponder, let us search out in them the deep lessons which they hold.

As we have said, the community gave scandal

to outsiders, and suffered within. Such conditions could not long exist without being reported to Father Renault. At first he was unwilling to credit these reports, caused, he thought, by the jealousy of malcontents.

But when complaints continued to be made, and with ever-increasing emphasis, the Father Provincial took steps to have Mother Thérèse come to him at Avignon, where he was for the time staying, that he might question her and learn what foundation there was for all these complaints.

Mother Thérèse obeyed the summons. Father Renault, very paternally and seeking only the greatest good "of that little infant whom he had already accepted when it was in its cradle," wished to question Mother Thérèse concerning the administration of Mme. de La Villeurnoy. That was wisdom on his part, human wisdom at least. Mother Thérèse believed it was the part of divine wisdom not to say anything, and she refused to answer the questions that were put to her, declaring that it was not for her to judge her superior.

The admirable discretion which she showed was permitted by God for a definite purpose. In spite of all the reasons Mother Thérèse had for speaking, she thought to do so would be a lack of that respect which she should have for the one who stood to her in the place of God.

And in all truth is it not a fine thing to see this woman, humiliated, deposed, all but rejected by Father Renault himself, refuse to tell the truth concerning that "Foundress" who had founded nothing—that religious set up as one who would restore everything, but who actually brought everything to the brink of ruin. A lengthy report to Father Renault would never have resulted in as much good to the future daughters of Mother Thérèse as did that one sentence, uttered decisively and emphatically: "I will say nothing, Reverend Father, about Mme. de La Villeurnoy." And the Reverend Father was considerate enough to respect her silence.

He himself went to La Louvesc to investigate. That investigation ended matters. Some days after its completion, the Bishop of Viviers deposed the superior and ordered a new election. The election was set for September 24th, the Feast of Our Lady of Mercy. Several of the sisters called attention to the day. The Bishop decided that an absolute majority of the votes cast would be necessary for election, and, before the election was held, he approved the selection of either Mother Thérèse or of a young Mother accepted some time previously by the Foundress, but actually in the house for but a few months—Mother Contenet. To her, by the humble, urgent advice of Mother Thérèse all the votes were given.[2]

God definitely showed that His Will was that His servant should henceforth dwell in the shadow.

Sad was the ending of this drama of eleven months. Madame de La Villeurnoy, to whom the Cenacle, curiously enough, had never given the title of Mother, withdrew from the Congregation. Subsequently she brought suit against the community, which was ordered to pay her a large sum of money.

What were the thoughts of Mother Thérèse in her silent retreat? None, assuredly, that were not wholly charitable.

It will be edifying to end this lamentable history with the judgment which, years afterwards, Mother Thérèse made on her who had supplanted her. "Madame de La Villeurnoy wished to do good and to contribute to the good of the community. When she was superior she evidenced her goodwill and her devotion. The poverty of the house opened the way every day to innumerable privations, and as nothing had been organized, she believed she had the power to do everything according to her own judgment." [3]

XIII. Heartbreaks

THE DAY when Mlle. Contenet entered the Saint Regis House, Mme. de La Villeurnoy could not refrain from expressing admiration for her to the community. "What a woman this postulant is!" she exclaimed.

In Mlle. Contenet God had indeed given to the Congregation of the Religious of the Retreat a sub-

ject of exceptional worth. Loyal, straightforward
in character, she could not but inspire feelings that
were wholly supernatural. And yet it was through
her that God was to impose still greater suffering
on Mother Thérèse, suffering that entered into
the deepest depths of her heart.

In a note written in 1864, Mother Thérèse tells
us of three crosses which God brought into her
life during the generalship of Mother Contenet.
"I witnessed," she says, "subjects dismissed whose
virtue I well knew: I was pictured to the diocesan
authority as one who always acted according to her
own feelings, without deferring to her ecclesiastical superiors: finally, even in the community itself, they thought I regretted not having any part
in the government of the community: they kept
me on the outside of everything, and always assigned me occupations that would keep me away
from recreation."

Such, substantially, is the recital in which the
humble Mother Thérèse recounted her agony to
her superior. Let us add at once, that the evening
of the very day she wrote these confidences, she
sought out her superior and said to her: "Mother,
I dare not go to Holy Communion tomorrow. I
was certainly lacking in charity in telling you all
those unnecessary things which are much better
forgotten. I beg you not to think of them again,
and never to speak of them. They would perhaps
give an unfavorable impression of those who have
been to me but the instruments of the good God." [1]

But Mother Thérèse had exaggerated nothing. If we do not know the facts which she had in mind when she speaks of the unkind reports made concerning her to the ecclesiastical authorities, we do know the details of the two other trials she recalls.

It is difficult to judge the decision of a superior seventy-five years after it was given. But time does not prevent our realizing the sharpness of the suffering which tested Mother Thérèse when she witnessed Mother Contenet dismiss, one by one, all the Choir Religious who had been her well-beloved daughters. One only escaped the tempest —Mother Joséphine Grégoire.[2] How plentiful the tears of the superior of yesterday as she saw go from her those whom she had received and moulded! With humility she excused such strange decisions. "These Mothers," she said, "did not seem to have that combination of qualities desirable for the Institute as it entered into this its new phase of life."

We will accept her judgment. In sharing her thoughts we may be sure of not violating the law of holy charity.

As for the third cross, it will be more difficult for us to explain it, at least to trace therein the special action of God.

Father Rigaud, Superior at La Louvesc, seeing Mother Thérèse one day, all alone about to dig a bed for vegetables, said to Mother Contenet who accompanied him: "What! is this the way you treat Mother Thérèse?"

PART THREE: *The Shadow*

The shadow had indeed grown dark over her in whom Father Terme had recognized "such good judgment and such discernment of souls as are rarely met with in a woman." The Foundress of the Cenacle was no longer invited to talk with her sisters during the time of recreation. At the best years of her life (she was about thirty-five) she, to whom they owed the house, the chapel and most of the customs of the community, was wilfully and deliberately given the tasks of washing pots and pans, of sweeping corridors, of weeding garden walks, of digging flower beds—all of which occupations would keep her apart from others.

The hidden life must have very great value in the Eyes of God since it pleased Him to permit a religious of Mother Thérèse's worth to be thus consumed by it!

May one venture to wonder what would have become of the Cenacle if its Foundress had governed it for a longer period than just those ten years? A human question, to which probably God would answer: The Cenacle would not have grown to be the flourishing order it is had not Mother Thérèse been humiliated and cast aside for nearly half a century. The more vigorous an oak tree is, the deeper down in the ground will its roots be buried.

And one may perhaps find a further reason for this disposition of Providence.

God founded the Religious of the Retreat to give the Spiritual Exercises of Saint Ignatius. Now, the Spiritual Exercises ought to lead us to a contempt of self, to a love of humiliation, to the third degree of humility. The Foundress of the order destined to extend those Exercises throughout the world should be the living expression of their ideal.

Henceforth, thinking of their Mother, always humiliated, always silent, misjudged, put to one side, deprived systematically of every office, her life hidden in the deepest humiliation, her daughters will be able to speak of that of which they know.

The Church urges the priest on the day of his ordination to imitate Him Whom he touches: *Imitamini quod tractatis.* Mother Thérèse imitated for forty years the Spiritual Exercises which she had conducted with tenderness and with love.

So long as the Cenacle lives, the Religious of the Retreat will find in the resigned silence of their Mother a living light to hand on to the souls God sends them—humility.

XIV. La Montée Saint-Barthélemy

MADEMOISELLE JARICOT, Foundress of the work of the Propagation of the Faith, had a sister, Mme. Perrin, whose daughter had for some time been a novice in the Saint Regis House at La Louvesc.

PART THREE: *The Shadow*

One day in the summer of 1841, Mme. Perrin disembarked at Tournon to make a retreat in that city. During the course of the Exercises she told Mother Contenet of her desire to see the new society established at Lyons.

How could one refuse to accept such a proposal? Some days later, Mme. Perrin departed from Tournon with the fixed intention of purchasing as soon as possible a suitable house wherein the Exercises of Saint Ignatius might be given. The opportunity she sought soon presented itself. "The house has been found and purchased," she sent back word to Mother Contenet. With all possible speed the Mother General betook herself to Lyons.[1]

The part played by Mother Thérèse in the history of the Fourvière foundation is too important not to recount it in detail. And the documents on the subject are very numerous.

First of all we give the story written by Mother de Larochenégly:

"I was chosen to accompany Mother Contenet. The month was December; the rain was falling in torrents, and we had a long way to go to reach the rue Sala, where the Jesuit Fathers, who had sent word they wished to see us on our arrival, had their house. Father Fouillot, always very paternal, had reserved a room for us in a house in the rue de la Sphère. But this house was so dirty that we dared not remove any of our clothing when we went to bed.

"The next day, we visited Fathers Maillard, the Provincial, Renault and Fouillot, in order to talk over with them the founding of the new house, a very large property, La Montée Saint-Barthélemy, near l'escalier des Chazeaux.

"Alas! at the first glance, the Mother General knew the Congregation could never establish itself there. What was to be done? Madame Perrin had purchased it in our name. If we did not take it, it would be left on her hands.

" 'Buy it,' said the Jesuit Fathers.

"Mother Contenet asked time to consider the matter. Finally she said with respectful firmness that she could not see her way to follow their counsel."

Reading the contemporary accounts, one sees that the refusal of Mother Contenet was not without merit, for in order to force her to comply the Father Provincial had said: "If you refuse, I will withdraw my Fathers."

"And I also will leave you," added Father Fouillot. Very much distressed, Mother Contenet replied: "As you will, Father. But I cannot do an injury to my Congregation. My conscience would not permit it."

Another document adds: "One might say she fought against heaven and against earth." Indeed, during the negotiations the daughters of Mlle. Jaricot were praying and keeping candles burning,

PART THREE: *The Shadow*

to the end that Mother Contenet would decide to
purchase the property.

In her perplexity Mother Contenet took the
matter to the Archbishop.

"Rent the house," said the Archbishop, "for five
years."

Cardinal de Bonald's advice was followed. Some
days later, Mother Contenet returned to Tournon.

Since the lease called for occupancy of the property by the springtime, the first Mothers and Sisters journeyed thereto on February 12th. When
they came to take possession, their first impression
was most unfavorable. Nevertheless, they set to
work to get things into some sort of condition in
the midst of all the hardships.

At the end of five days, Mother Contenet sent
for further assistance. In response, two more sisters
arrived by the boat.[2]

Since there was question of only humble and
obscure offices, one is not surprised to learn that
one of these two sisters was Mother Thérèse. She
came, according to the intention of her superiors,
to wash floors, sweep the stairs, make the beds. In
reality, God sent her to Lyons that she might purchase the Cenacle of Fourvière and found the
house wherein, forty years later, she was to die.

Only in two other instances will God show to
those who did not know her the things of which
Mother Thérèse was capable. Then she will sink
again into her beloved obscurity.

[107]

There were now seven of them at the Maison des Chazeaux. Indeed, every day proved more clearly the wisdom of Mother Contenet's refusal. Poorly laid out, sombre-looking, cheerless, damp, with no view, and with a canal running through the garden, the property acquired by Mme. Perrin could never be made into a house suitable for the accommodation of the women who would come for the Spiritual Exercises.

They tried it, nevertheless. Towards the feast of the Ascension, when all was as nearly in suitable condition as it could be, the Reverend Mother decided to schedule a retreat.

As was proper, she asked aid of the Fathers of the rue Sala. She was therein very unfortunate. For reasons unknown to us, the Fathers all made themselves scarce. The following pointed sentences, written by Mother Thérèse, are not without relish.

"As we insisted that we must have a Jesuit, one of the Fathers said: 'Get a volume of Bourdaloue: you will find there sermons ready made.' This answer so affected Mother Contenet, that she, in spite of her firmness, could not restrain her tears.

"Our distress, however, did effectively appeal to Father Maillard. He sent us Father Nampon to preach the retreat. Twenty women attended it."

Very ill-advised was the Father who had referred them so cavalierly to Bourdaloue. God had His own special designs with regard to that retreat.

During those days of recollection and of divine favors, Mmes. Burtin and Garnier conjointly conceived the idea of the great work of the Ladies of Calvary.

Few retreats were so fruitful as this first one at Lyons given by the daughters of Father Terme. Mother Thérèse was, of course, scarcely in evidence; but who can say that the light and grace which were to give birth to the Ladies of Calvary were not due to her, to her prayers, to her sacrifice?

After that retreat, the house at Lyons was established. Mother Contenet departed, leaving Mother Thérèse, with a few sisters, to take care of the house.

Towards the following October, Mother Joséphine Grégoire joined them. For more than two years, courageous Mother Thérèse dwelt, without the benefit of sunlight, behind these walls dripping humidity, finding, no doubt, these dark rooms and corridors more in keeping with her hidden life than La Louvesc, where through the many windows the sunlight entered at will.

"I have frequently heard her say," wrote Sister Regis, "that this time seemed to her very long, forasmuch as she remained there alone with Sister Marie for eighteen months. God alone knows all that our venerated Mother suffered at this period of her life. In her poverty she cultivated the garden, from which she drew almost all the nourishment she had."

So, again we see Mother Thérèse bent all day long over the vegetable beds, digging, seeding, weeding and watering them.

A singular occupation, surely, for the foundress of an order, whose whole heart was set on the glory of God!

But the hour draws near when this rough working woman will for twenty-four hours lay aside her spade, and in the course of one day, by her decision, her intelligent ability, her energy, endow her beloved Congregation with one of the most beautiful of all its houses—the Cenacle of Fourvière.

XV. The Rôle of the Little Hunchback

ONE DAY when Mother Contenet was on her way to Lyons, she entered a goldsmith's shop at the Place Saint-Côme in order to have some profession crosses repaired. This goldsmith, named Pasquier, had been recommended to Mother Contenet as a very honest man. He was very short of stature, and a hunchback. M. Pasquier surprised the Mother General not a little when, without any preliminaries, he said to her: "I know, Madame, that you are here for the purpose of securing a house. The one you have rented is not suitable for your purpose, and I advise you not to purchase it."

Greatly astonished, but accustomed to see in all things the Hand of God, Mother Contenet thanked this unknown goldsmith for being so kind as to show interest in her work, and asked him if he knew of a suitable property.

"I have such a one for sale," he answered. "It is on the plateau of Fourvière. You can see if it is suitable. If it is not, we will search for another."

The property he spoke of proved too small and too far away from the church. Mother Contenet was considering whether or not to refuse it, when God freed her from her uncertainty.

A devout priest, an epileptic, often came accompanied by his housekeeper to pray in the chapel of Chazeaux. This priest was a close friend of M. Pasquier, and learning from him that the Religious of the Retreat desired to purchase a house, he told his friend of a large property situated near the chapel of Fourvière, with a vineyard and two groups of buildings. Prior to 1793 the entire estate belonged to the municipality, but since then had been sold several times. The people were accustomed to call it the "Roman Forum." It was here that in the days of the Terror a devout widow had hidden the miraculous statue of Fourvière under a heap of vine branches.

Pleased with the information given him by the good canon, M. Pasquier conveyed it in turn to Mother Contenet, who, at an appointed time, went with M. Pasquier and the sisters to look at the property.

"Too large, and too fine for us," said Mother Contenet. "Our circumstances will not allow us to purchase such a property. I do not believe the good God wishes to give us this dwelling place."

"O woman of little faith," answered M. Pasquier, "Lyons is a city of resources. The people here will help you. As for myself, I pledge you two thousand frances to pay the interest."

His words carried such assurance, that Mother Contenet directed the goldsmith to take charge of the matter. Some days later, he returned with the terms set by the owner, M. Duchamp. The price was one hundred and eighty thousand francs.

"We cannot buy at such a price," said Mother Contenet; and, very much disappointed, she departed for La Louvesc.

In spite of the precautions taken that nothing should be known of the transaction, Mme. Perrin and Mlle. Jaricot heard of it. Mother Thérèse, who was now alone at Lyons, learned, through the indiscreet talk of a servant, that Mme. Perrin was coming up to Lyons the next day to buy this house of M. Duchamp. What was to be done?

She could send word to Mother Contenet to come at once, but there was no possible hope that she could arrive in time. Was it not necessary to handle the business even though Mother Contenet were not there?

Mother Thérèse resolved to leave it all to Divine Providence.

During that night she felt herself supernaturally driven to conclude the purchase.

The Saints readily recognize Divine action. The next morning Mother Thérèse rang the bell at the house of the goldsmith. She was rudely sent away, for M. Pasquier was not yet out of bed. But a rebuff could never in the world discourage Mother Thérèse. She went away, and she returned. This time the goldsmith received her. The whole matter was put before him.

M. Pasquier realized that haste was imperative. He went to the owner, took him in turn to the house of the notary, M. Berloty, had the bill of sale drawn up, and secured at a lower price—one hundred and forty-eight thousand francs. Then he came back to find Mother Thérèse.

"Do you wish to purchase the property?" he asked. Without hesitating she answered, "Yes." She felt herself, it seems, irresistibly impelled to make that answer.

Some hours later, Mother Contenet arrived, distraught by a night of travel, and even more by the most painful forebodings concerning the house, with whose purchase the future of the Congregation seemed to her to be bound up.

"What has happened?" she said as soon as she saw Mother Thérèse.

For answer the latter showed her the bill of sale.

The Reverend Mother was moved beyond words. She seized the hand of Mother Thérèse, and, crying for joy, said, "Blessed be God!" Then she added these words, which speak volumes in regard to her opinion of the poor humiliated one: "And it was actually *you* who purchased this house!"

Yes, it was indeed she who purchased it. And God had not permitted her to do so without reason; just as He had a definite purpose in permitting those words to fall from the lips of the Mother General.

Mother Thérèse, whose discriminating soul and sensitive heart could discern every shade of meaning, experienced somewhat of a shock at this strange sort of thanks! But what does thanks matter to the humble? Long ago all their spirituality was summed up in those words of Saint John the Baptist: "I must decrease" (John iii. 30).

The little hunchback of the Place Saint-Côme— also one of the humble—some days later was offered ten thousand francs if he would secure a re-selling of this property. He refused.

One day when the Mother General was expressing her gratitude to him, he answered her in this unlooked-for way: "I think of you more than you imagine. Just a little while ago when making my adoration at Saint-Nizier, it was your work that I had in mind all the time."

A poor hunchback, up to that time unknown, a poor religious, called from Tournon to scrub floors and walls—such were the instruments which God used to transform this "Roman Forum," as they called it, into a vast house of prayer.

Divine ways are ever the same—to bring to naught the wisdom of the wise, to overthrow the learning of the learned, to conquer life through death, to overcome power by weakness. The Fourvière Cenacle is the work of one forsaken, yea of one despised. . . .

Is not this the reason why it has up to this day weathered every storm? This House of Prayer is founded not upon sand, but upon the humiliation of one of God's elect.

XVI. On the Hill of Fourvière

THE HOUSE at Fourvière having been purchased, Mother Thérèse went back into obscurity. For almost twelve years she led the hidden life of a religious to whom superiors seemingly wished to assign manual labors rather than those of apostolic character.

It would be tedious to tell of her goings and her comings. Tournon, La Louvesc, Crémieu, Lyons saw her in turn at various times.

It was at Lyons, however, that she passed the greater part of the twelve years whose story we are about to write—a very monotonous story, but a most edifying one, as we shall see.

The former owners of the property recently purchased reserved the right to dwell thereon for two years. As soon as the house was unoccupied, Mother Thérèse and her companions began to move in. Early one morning, before the sun had risen, they filled a small hand-cart with the household effects and painfully climbed the steep hill to the Fourvière estate.

One is edified as one reads the story of those hard climbs, recorded by Mother Joséphine.

"In order to keep down expenses, we ourselves undertook the task of conveying the household effects from one house to the other. Many times during the day did we climb that holy hill, in the morning before dawn, and in the evening at nightfall, in order that we might not meet anyone. Although we would arrive quite worn out, it was, nevertheless, necessary to work hard, for the rooms were even filthier, if that were possible, than those at La Montée Saint-Barthélemy.

"Moreover, it was Lent, and we did not dispense ourselves readily from the laws of the Church, so although we started to wash the walls and the floors as soon as we got up in the morning, we remained fasting until noon. When the dinner bell sounded, we were so tired that we found it almost impossible to eat even the meager meal which we had carried with us.

"After some months of this work, the house was finally ready to receive the little community, of which Mother de Larochenégly had been named superior."

So wrote Mother Grégoire.

For the first time since her deposition, Mother Thérèse held an office—that of assistant. But let us not deceive ourselves. If the assistant is, in the Cenacle, the authority immediately below the superior, her chief charge is the supervision of material labors, and by that very fact she had as her portion the more exacting and difficult drudgeries. We may add that, since the Fourvière community numbered six, Mother Thérèse seldom had occasion to come out of the shadow. She continued deeply hidden therein.

Of this whole period not one letter from her has come down to us. Yet some few words of hers, which have the brevity of a diary entry, enable us to know her life then as one of privation and suffering.

"At Lyons we did not meet with the charitable aid which M. Pasquier had led us to expect. The house had to be paid for; and the Congregation was still overburdened with the old indebtedness. Moreover, we had much to suffer in the matter of food, of clothing, and of living quarters. Wheat being so dear, we did not hesitate to gather up the remnants of black bread which the gardener did not wish to keep and which he threw alongside the convent wall. We ourselves made the mattresses, the coverlets, and other things necessary for the house. At night and in the early morning a single lamp was all the light the community had. It was placed in the corridor on which our cells opened; we had, therefore, to dress in semi-darkness. At recreation we would work by such a poor light that many of us have impaired sight as a consequence.

"Two full years after the blessing of the chapel, we were still without the means of securing a ciborium. The only sacred vessel that we had was a small chalice, the paten of which was used in giving Holy Communion. Imagine our joy, therefore, when Father Deschamps brought us a small silver-plated ciborium, the gift of Mme. d'Agoust of Grenoble. A little later, Mme. de Sermaize, of Paray-le-Monial, and one of the Hospitallers Sisters of Saint Charles conjointly donated an ostensorium to replace the pewter one which up to that time had served us for Benediction. The first flower vases that we had were given to us at the request of Father Laurent, and Mme. de Saint-Cyr sent us two long garlands of white roses which for several years served as the best ornament which our altar had.

"Finally, to celebrate the blessing of the chapel, Mme. Perret, of Saint-Étienne, gave us a small organ, which for a long time remained silent because we had no organist." [1]

Mother de Larochenégly confirms with her authority as Superior General these records of Mother Thérèse.

"The first six years at Fourvière," she says, "were

spent laboriously in furnishing the house.[2] The older Mothers (we speak of Mothers Thérèse and Joséphine), accustomed as they were to work and to every sort of privation, gave to the little community an atmosphere of fervor, of regularity, which I recall with the greatest happiness. No other of our houses had to meet such conditions of poverty and sacrifice, nor could have accepted them with greater courage. The less desirable products of the garden were the only vegetables that came to our table; the better kind were reserved for the retreatants, or were sold. As during the whole of Lent our meals consisted of stewed fruit and a salad of herbs and potatoes, we thought we would make a special occasion of Easter Day by serving pot-au-feu. This drew down on our Mother Procurator a sharp rebuke from Father de Jocas, who urged the community to cultivate a spirit more in accordance with that of Saint Ignatius, adding that Providence would surely come to our aid and free us from our material difficulties."

This page written by Mother de Larochenégly gives us a very clear idea of what the life of our venerable Foundress must have been during these first years at Fourvière: a life of austerity, of labor, of mortification and obscurity.

God, Who never lets Himself be outdone in generosity, willed to give most sensible evidences of His good-will to the Religious of the Cenacle of Lyons, who for His sake lived these months and years of extreme poverty.

The records tell us that during these years of privation the doctor never once had occasion to enter the house. Moreover, in the dark days of the revolution of 1848 the Convent of the Cenacle was the only one spared by those who were termed the "vultures."

Mother de Larochenégly records that, some weeks before the revolution, a saintly woman who was making a retreat at the Cenacle Convent said to her: "Soon a storm of destruction and of evil will break over Lyons. But do not fear; I have seen the Blessed Virgin blessing your house and Saint Joseph enveloping it with his mantle." Her prophecy proved true to the letter. Since that day the statue of Saint Joseph which protected the house remains an object of great veneration. Many favors have been obtained through his intercession, and the Cenacle of Lyons gives him in gratitude the title of "Founder."

XVII. Humility Triumphant

WHILE THE house of Lyons was being established, Providence brought Father Fouillot from the north of France to the vicinity of La Louvesc. His superiors had assigned him to Notre-Dame d'Ay as spiritual director of the Fathers making their tertianship.

PART THREE: *The Shadow*

Because of this physical proximity, he was able to labor more in the spiritual moulding of the novices of the Congregation. A note taken from the archives of the Cenacle tells us: "Father Fouillot divided his time almost equally between the work of directing his own religious and ours. On feast days he came to hear confessions and to preach to our little community. Each and every one was the object of his care. This good Father had at his command a thousand different ways of arousing zeal and of carrying novices into the spirit of the other world. Moreover, his direction while strong, was at the same time very paternal, so that the novices said among themselves: "Father Fouillot is too much occupied with the Blessed Virgin and with the Cenacle to have any time to scold us." [1]

The Cenacle! This title which was to be given to the Institute as its final and characteristic name, was an inspiration given by God to Father Fouillot some time prior to 1847.

Apropos of this, Father Fouillot himself wrote: "The work of giving retreats ought to have a title which shows its object and the need which justifies it. No title seems better suited to these aims than the title of 'Our Lady of the Retreat in the Cenacle.' Jesus Christ on ascending into heaven said to His disciples: 'Stay you in the city, till you be endued with power from on high.'" (Luke xxiv. 49.)

Then, as the Acts of the Apostles tell us, they

returned from the Mount of Olives to Jerusalem and enclosed themselves in the Cenacle, and there persevered with one mind in prayer with the holy women and Mary the Mother of Jesus.

Later, Father Fouillot, in a still celebrated letter which he wrote to Mother Thérèse, reverts to this subject which was so dear to him. "The wording of the form for the taking of the vows, which I am drawing up for you," he said, "I found in that last prayer of Our Divine Master, offered in the Cenacle, wherein He asks for His disciples: 'Holy Father, keep them in Thy name; . . . that they may be one, as we also are' (John xvii. 11). And if it may be permitted me to add to this desire of Our Saviour some other particular desires which I believe to be according to His Heart, I would beg your entire Congregation ever to hold in mind and ever to practise what Our Blessed Lord said, and what He did, in the Cenacle, to make it your true school—a school wherein the only contest will be to abase oneself and to raise up others, as illustrated in the example of Jesus Christ at the feet of Saint Peter, and in the example of Blessed Mary taking the last place among the holy women—an example which your vocation will lead you to imitate. I pray this divine Mother of Grace and Humility to grant you her peace, as a mother to her children, and to cause to descend upon you all in abundance the Seven Gifts of the Holy Spirit, which she possesses in their fulness, and of which she has the merciful dispensation."

The name chosen, therefore, bespeaks an entire program of action. It shows the road which thereafter the daughters of Father Terme and Mother Thérèse would follow. To Father Fouillot belongs the credit of this decision.

But the Cenacle owes him more than this. The young novices of La Louvesc were indeed inspired when they said that he was much occupied with the work of the Cenacle.

The documents of that period tell us that Father Fouillot was directed by his Provincial to write the Rule of the Society. It will not be without interest to note here the very clear vision which the Director of the tertianship Fathers had in these first days concerning the future of the Cenacle. He wrote in a letter to Mother Thérèse:

"When I accepted the task of forming the Congregation, I told you that I would not accept the charge if I had not already seen that it was to be widely extended. You will remember that at the small gathering at La Louvesc I spoke to you as if we already had houses at Lyons and Paris. All your sisters had been trained in the thought of devoting themselves to extending the work, that its good purpose might be widely propagated. We have in view, therefore, not a local congregation, but a congregation with numerous houses, and according to this view your Constitutions have been drawn up."

These Constitutions we know were the work of his heart.[2] However, Father Fouillot did not wish to make anything definitely rigid. He wished to try out the instrument which he had forged, reserving to himself the right to modify any portion if a greater good demanded it. Only this reservation can explain the strange measures which he took when the sudden death of Mother Contenet, in 1852, made necessary the election of a new superior general. We are compelled here to record a mistake made by Father Fouillot; but before doing so we would like to answer a question which has perhaps come to the mind of some of our readers: What did Father Fouillot think of Mother Thérèse? A passage from a letter written by him to Mother Thérèse in January, 1855, some months before her great trial, throws light upon the matter: "I repeat to you, Reverend Mother, what I have often said at different times to your community: the remembrance they should bear in their hearts of all that you did at the beginning of this work, and of the agonies that you suffered in all their vicissitudes."

These words show the veneration he had for Mother Thérèse. They show, moreover, that ofttimes he advised the Religious of the Cenacle to have a real cult for her and a profound admiration. It is but just before we come to tell of the trials which, without intending it, Father Fouillot caused the Cenacle, to recall all the good which through his good-will he had accomplished.

Madame Anaïs was Assistant General and Mistress of Novices at the house in the rue du Regard in Paris when the unexpected death of Mother Contenet, Superior General, took place. Although gifted with high qualities, among them, doubtless, a desire to do good, Mme. Anaïs had, unfortunately, a very active imagination which made it impossible for her to give a balanced judgment on anything. We may add that her piety was rather external than real. Saint Ignatius would perhaps have numbered her in the class of those courageous ones who devote themselves whole-souledly to work, but he would never have counted her, according to our judgment, among the number of those who follow Jesus Christ covered with shame. However, Mother Contenet had placed her confidence in Mme. Anaïs, and had entrusted to her the responsibility of training the novices. As to Father Fouillot, he always saw in her a chosen soul, called to extraordinary heights of prayer. Nothing could change his opinion in this respect—neither the irregularities of conduct which shocked some members of the community, nor the peculiar habit of talking constantly of her pretended extraordinary spiritual experiences. We must indeed believe that this religious was unusually clever; how otherwise explain how a woman of Mother Contenet's worth and a man such as Father Fouillot could have been so misled? However, it is possible that God permitted these things for our good.

When one sees a spiritual director of the tertianship of the Society of Jesus, knowing thoroughly the rules drawn up by Saint Ignatius for the discerning of spirits, knowing all the devices of the angel of darkness, yet allowing himself to be deceived to such a degree, one is forced to admit how easy it is to become the victim of him who once was the light-bearer.

The Mother General was dead. Some days afterwards the question of the elections was to be settled. Without any indirectness, in fact quite openly, Father Fouillot advised the sisters to elect Mme. Anaïs. Moreover, wishing to provide for every contingency, he asked the Mothers who had any chance of being elected to pledge themselves not to accept the superiorship for more than three years, instead of the ten years for which the Constitutions called. Thanks to this measure, Mme. Anaïs in case of defeat now would have a possible chance of being elected seven years sooner.

The election was held on March 7th.

The Superior of Lyons, Mother de Larochenégly, received the majority of the votes.

This election was a great disappointment to Father Fouillot; and, always convinced that Mme. Anaïs exercised a dominant influence in the Cenacle, he made the further mistake of declaring her co-Foundress.

The inevitable followed. Some of the religious of the house in Paris made common cause with Mme. Anaïs. Immediately unity was broken, and the worst was to be feared.

* * *

PART THREE: *The Shadow*

Up to this time, Mother Thérèse had been content to pray unto God, seeking her strength in silence and confidence. Doubt for her was no longer possible. The work so dear to her heart was threatened with ruin; therefore she came forth from the shadow. Recalling other days and the far-seeing kindness of Father Renault, she decided to send out to him that last appeal in a storm: "Save us, we perish!" Here is her letter, dated February 13, 1855:

"REVEREND FATHER:

"Many years have passed since I have had the honor of writing to you. During those years, what things have happened in this our dear Congregation! What suffering, what tribulation have assailed it! You know, since you have shared its sufferings with paternal and unfailing devotion. But have they ended? Alas! the cross which weighs upon our work at this moment is perhaps the heaviest that we have ever borne.

"How lamentable it is, Reverend Father, to see those who wish to do the very greatest good to the work, really harm it; and this because they are not willing to be enlightened. . . . It is astonishing that those so serious-minded, so highly placed, so holy, should permit themselves to be deceived. We know not what will be the outcome of this unfortunate business. Bishop Guibert, who is informed of everything, has been good enough to take charge of the matter. Cardinal Bonald is also

very good to us. His Eminence is to confer with
the Bishop of Viviers in order to decide everything.
We await these decisions in peace, and we shall be
respectfully submissive, persuaded that the Will of
God will be shown to us through the instrument of
our highest superiors. Bishop Guibert has ordered
that all of the professed of the Congregation meet
at Lyons. He has set the first week of Lent as
the time of the meeting, and His Excellency has
kindly consented to preside. The annual retreat
will be held at the same time. We do not know as
yet who is the Father who will give us the retreat;
but we know that it will not be you, Reverend
Father, as we had dared to hope. It would have
been a great pleasure to all of us, and above all to
our Reverend Mother, to be able to profit by your
counsels in such painful circumstances as these.
But no matter what anyone may say, you are none
the less the Father of our Congregation. To you it
was willed by testament, by him who did not live
long enough to complete his plan, and who during
his life looked upon you as his Superior and his
Father. And Bishop Bonnel, the Bishop of Viviers,
also recommended and confided it to you. All this
I will declare at the proper time, both to those
who do not know it and to those who pretend not
to know it and would thereby deceive the Congregation at the present moment. . . .

"Pardon my having written at such length. . . .
Here we speak to no one of our suffering, for we

wish that everyone should ever remain ignorant of it.

"Before I close this letter, permit me to beg of you to be pleased to accept the expression of my well-deserved and sincere gratitude; first, for all that I owe you personally, and then for all that you have done and suffered for this little Congregation. It will ever be dear to you because it has cost you so much. It will always, I trust, have a claim on your good-will and your protection.

"Be kind enough to accept the assurance of the profound respect with which I have the honor to be, Reverend Father,

"Your very humble and obedient daughter,

"Thérèse,

"*Religious of the Retreat.*"

This is the letter of one who dwells in silence, who has taken the time to weigh the consequences of passing events. It is also the spontaneous cry of a soul. The Saints are always themselves, and Mother Thérèse practised no artifices of speech; hence, respectfully but firmly, she tells the whole truth.

Father Renault shows in his reply that he thought as she did.

"Reverend Mother and very dear Daughter:

"Peace to you, and the love of Our Lord.

"Your letter which I have received is a consolation to me in the midst of all that I feel at this moment. Oh, if they had but believed me! But

God has permitted all this for the good of all your members and in order more strongly to unite your Congregation. The wind that blows the trees forces the roots to take firmer hold. I have ever desired that the Congregation have its own government— govern itself under the authority of the Bishop of Viviers. I have said this and repeated it on every occasion. I would publish it from the house-tops. Of the two evils, it will be better for all that the infant be allowed to suffer some falls which will not injure its health rather than forever to try to prevent its walking alone.

"Take your place behind your Superior. Be a consolation to this poor Mother. Pray; have confidence. Tell the Bishop and the Cardinal absolutely everything. Your Congregation is in a difficult situation—extraordinary, unique. The Superior alone cannot free the Congregation from it; it is for the Bishop of Viviers to come to the fore, and for you to say to him—as the Apostles to Our Lord, terrified as they were in the storm—'Lord, save us!'

"The holy Bishop will, in the presence of God, consider the matter, will give his decision . . . and I trust that calm will be restored. From all this discord should result a great lesson, and it is my earnest wish that the Congregation may profit by it for all time.

"Kindly give my respects to your Reverend Mother. May God strengthen her soul. Greetings from your former Father to all.

"I thank you for your letter, and I ask you to believe in the sentiments of respect, of esteem and affection in Our Lord with which you have ever inspired me from the very beginning, and with which I remain always, my good and beloved daughter,

"Your humble and devoted servant,

"FRANCIS RENAULT, S.J."

Some days after the reception of this letter, that is to say in the beginning of March, the retreat which Mother Thérèse had desired Father Renault to give was held at Lyons. All the Mothers took part in it. But before the retreat was ended, Mother de Larochenégly made an unexpected decision. Did she perchance act for Bishop Guibert in the matter? Or was it Father Renault who was back of the decision?

We do not know. But on a certain morning Mother Thérèse departed for Paris. She had received a twofold order which she was to carry out there: first, to see that the novitiate was transferred to Lyons according to the wish of the Mother General; and then to act as counselor to Mme. Anaïs, who when the retreat was finished returned to Paris as Superior. How delicate was this double rôle for Mother Thérèse! Madame Anaïs had just suffered a defeat of which she could not but be sensible; and, secondly, the training of the novices had been taken out of her hands. What ability, what gentle firmness would Mother

A Great and Humble Soul

Thérèse be compelled to employ in order to resist successfully, without in any way crushing, the disposition of her who constantly called herself co-Foundress. That delicacy and that firmness Mother Thérèse knew how to exercise after the manner of the Saints. All the same, we must admit that it is a sufficiently challenging situation that there should be living in the same house she who having founded everything wished to remain unknown, and she who having founded nothing, paraded a title which in no way belonged to her.

* * *

It was not long before Mother Thérèse had to take account of the gravity of the situation. The five or six members who made up the community at Paris were nearly all of them openly on Mme. Anaïs' side, and the Coadjutor Sisters were actively solicited to take sides with her. Without hesitation, Mother Thérèse decided first and at all costs to save the Sisters. She therefore stooped to these little ones, and by her counsels, her remonstrances, her appeals, succeeded in keeping them on the right road. Not one of them lost her vocation. One can hear Mother Thérèse speaking in their noble reply to all the advances which were made to them: "We can never make a mistake in remaining under obedience to our superiors."

But the real danger of the Congregation lay in the wilfulness of the Choir Religious. Prayer alone

could save the Cenacle. Mother Thérèse prayed.
Her prayer was victorious, but after many trials.

Bishop Guibert, believing it necessary to study
the situation personally, comes to Paris. He interviews each Mother at length, and gauges the stub-
bornness of her resistance. In his judgment there
is but one way out; he takes it: Mme. Anaïs, who
had spoken of leaving, he permits to depart from
the Congregation, and he names in her place as
Superior of the house, Mother Thérèse. One can
imagine the agonies which this humble Mother
suffered while Mme. Anaïs delayed her departure
for so many days. It called for all the supernatural
grace that Mother Thérèse could command to face
the difficulties arising from the continued presence
of her who no longer was a part of the Cenacle.

Thanks to a letter which Mother Thérèse wrote
at this time to Mother de Larochenégly, we can
bring to life again some part of the Calvary that
she suffered.

"MY REVEREND MOTHER:

"I regret to say that Bishop Guibert has met
with more opposition than he expected. He has
met with it even from those who but lately declared that they would submit. . . . I am immensely
impressed by his goodness and his patience, although it is very evident that he is pained by such
obstinacy. It has been definitely decided that Mme.
Anaïs is to leave; the other four have not yet finally

said what they will do. They consider; they consult. They are allowed to do this so that they may
never be able to say that they were not free. . . .

"My strength fails me, and I shall not much
longer be able to endure such anguish as this; yet
my courage and my confidence are the same as
ever, and even were all the others to leave, I would
remain here to care for the house. . . . Let us place
everything in God's Hands and pray for those who
afflict our hearts with such sorrows. God alone can
bring them to a right mind.

"How sad will be our Feast of Saint Regis in
Paris! I fervently hope that those who are with
you, Reverend Mother, may make up to you in
joy for the sad news which it is my pain to write
you. May Saint Regis obtain for us the grace that
by that time I may have something more consoling
to tell you. In the meanwhile I repeat my *Parce
Domine,* in the fear that this storm has been
caused by my sins. . . ."

What calmness, what humility, yet withal what
firmness! One might imagine onself listening to
the captain of a ship whose vessel is about to
founder and who declares that he will remain at
his post even to the end.

The last sentence shows us even more clearly
than the rest the depths of this beautiful soul:
Mother Thérèse finds the cause of all this trouble
in her own sins.

The little community of Paris offers us a striking picture during that festival week in the octave of Corpus Christi, and anniversary of the festival week of Paray-le-Monial.

On the one side are the religious who have been deceived by the angel of darkness; on the other, a humble soul striking her breast, believing she is the blameworthy one, yet by her humility saving the community. The five unruly ones having departed, the heavenly peace of God entered into the souls of the others.

It might be feared that the happenings in Paris would be reëchoed in the other houses. But such was not the case. All the Religious of the Cenacle made their own those words of the Coadjutor Sisters, persuaded that while they remained obedient they could not be deceived; and more loyally than ever before, they gathered around the Mother General. The Cenacle was never again shaken by such a tempest. Fructified by this trial, it soon became one of the most flourishing Congregations of the Church.

As to Mother Thérèse, her mission as savior being ended, she again withdrew into the shadow, leaving the superiorship of the Paris house to one of the Mothers who had come from Lyons. All of which is evidence that in the designs of God the light was not to be withdrawn from under the bushel save just when it was needed to guide the daughters on the right road and to show them the dangers of the way.

To make the history complete, we will add that

three of the dissenters returned to the Congregation. Soon we will see Mother Thérèse showing herself especially affectionate towards one of them and striving for many months to plant in her bruised heart something of the virtue which filled her own.

XVIII. The True Mother

ONE EVENING in November, at eight o'clock, the little community at Tournon heard the sound of the door-bell. Great was the surprise of the sisters when they saw Mother Thérèse enter. Mother de Larochenégly, having decided to sell the Tournon house, had entrusted that commission to the Foundress, whom at the same time she named superior of that community. Superior! This was the first time since the far-off days of trial that Mother Thérèse came forth from the shadow and had confided to her by the Mother General some of her children. In Paris, one will recall, she had been named superior by Bishop Guibert.

That November evening, peace and happiness entered the Tournon Cenacle . . . and if the surprise was great (Mother Thérèse's coming had not been announced), great also was the joy of all those

PART THREE: *The Shadow*

hearts as they brightened under the warm rays of
this sun of goodness.

A true mother had just been given by God to
this happy Cenacle.

It is that Mother whom we would study. . . . It
is her heart that we must seek to understand. . . .

Mother Thérèse came only to put through the
sale of the house. As a matter of fact, however, it
was not by her that the sale was completed, and
her superiorship lasted but a few months. We believe that of her short rule we have said all when
we summarize it in the one word, "Goodness."

This goodness resembled—very remotely, of
course, but nevertheless truly—the goodness of the
good God. At least, her contemporaries took to
themselves the privilege of making that comparison. In what follows we will see that if this goodness allowed its warmth to shine upon all, it was
neither enfeebling nor indulgent; we will see that
if this Mother gave the fulness of her heart to her
children, that heart was one penetrated with abnegation and with sacrifice.

It seems that Mother Thérèse always knew when
a soul had need of her, and knew the remedy for
every sorrow that needed consolation.

"One day," a young religious tells us, "she met
me while I was carrying too heavy a load of wood.
She forthwith barred the passage-way, forced me to
put down half of my burden, and then she herself
took what she could of it. As she went away she

said to me, 'Now, make a fire that will last well, not one that will simply flame up.' "

In this case it was a question of relieving tired shoulders; but it was much more often souls before whose need she would stand, barring the passage for them also and obliging them to share with her half of their sorrow.

How many of the afflictions of others did she bear, this Mother whom they called the silent Mother, she who never spoke, but who was a pillar of support to all.[1]

With regard to this support, a sister came to her for comfort during a great storm. The Mother received the poor trembling child in her arms; she was too well acquainted with all distress to be astonished at this particular form. Meanwhile she tried to cure her of this somewhat childish fear. "My child," she said sweetly, "do you really believe that God could not find you if He willed that you should be struck by lightning? Do you think I could prevent Him from doing so? We should commit ourselves into His Hands. We are but His small creatures." "Since then," said the sister, "I have never again been afraid of lightning."

Once, having learned that a novice had lost father and mother, she went to her, called her her godchild because Thérèse was her name, and placing a medal of the Blessed Virgin around her neck said, "Behold her who will henceforth be your mother." And she looked at the orphan with such penetrating kindness that fifty years later that

orphan still held in her heart the memory of those
eyes.

Other storms shook the souls of her daughters.
. . . God has never permitted His elect to pitch
their tent upon Thabor. To those in trials the
Superior spoke the word of God, and there is often
a veritable tract of spirituality in her words of
confidence: "You suffer because you are humiliated. . . . Accustom yourself to make use of God at
such times. He dwells within you in order that you
may do so. Tell Him everything: He has the time
to listen to you. Say to Him, that you may console
Him, 'Grant me the grace to love to be despised,
that I may resemble Thee at least in some small
way.' "

It is easy to see by these vigorous counsels that
Mother Thérèse's piety was not sentimental: "Our
beloved retreat (that of the community) ended this
morning. To my mind, it was good, very good,
strong and forceful. We heard of perfection in its
highest degree: A religious ought to be wholly
God's; for that end there must be consecration,
sacrifice, abnegation, death to everything except
God. This doctrine suited me perfectly. I took delight in hearing it because it is my own manner of
thinking. I met again and again with the echo of
my own sentiments and my own dispositions. I was
glad, too, for the sake of the others, because I
thought that their souls would receive light from
what was said."

One day at recreation some of the novices spoke

of how uncomfortable the kneeling benches were. "Then," said Mother Thérèse, "we no longer wish to mortify ourselves; we must find another way of going to heaven." With Mother Thérèse everything was founded on the cross, whether that cross was large or small.

"The good God will carry out His work in the Cenacle, but amid adversities."

"After all, the religious life is a sufficiently great grace even though one purchase it at the price of the most difficult of sacrifices."

"Suffering, the bread of the strong, is not always to our liking. Nevertheless, it is necessary that we nourish ourselves thereon as long as the good God wills it."

"The cross, in whatsoever form it is presented to us, is ever the tree of life, and the hope which faith gives us of gathering fruit therefrom, renews in us the courage to accept it, with all its severities, from the Hand of Our Saviour, who has Himself chosen that one which will contribute most effectively to our sanctification.

"The cross is the gift which usually He bestows on His best friends. It is more precious than we think. We will understand its value later.

"Let us embrace the cross, howsoever it be given to us. You know it sanctifies whatever it touches, for it has been sanctified by Him Who is the source of all sanctity. Let us love it, if we can, for the more one loves it, the more profitable it is."

This strong spirituality never allowed, moreover, any let-up in sacrifice.

"My daughter, you would make a good begging
Sister in a mendicant order, or, perhaps, a Saint
Jeremias. Requests and lamentations abound in
your good and welcome letters. I take the greatest
interest in all your sufferings and in all the martyr-
doms that you tell me you have already suffered;
all the same, to my mind you are not so greatly to
be pitied, for your triple martyrdom will neces-
sarily enrich you by three palms and three crowns.
Such glories are not to be despised.

"However, I can hardly believe that these mar-
tyrdoms can have been as grievous as those of the
holy ones to whom you dare to compare yourself—
Saint Peter, Saint Andrew, and their good Master,
Who is also ours. They did not get off as easily as
you, for it cost them their lives; but you, we are
glad to say, have survived your tortures. May God
be blessed for that, and may He deign to grant
you the grace to profit from these little pin-pricks
which we experience on our way, while we wait to
be made worthy to suffer heavier blows."

A sister who more frequently than the others
recommended herself to the prayers of Mother
Thérèse, received this answer: "I think you are
like that religious who came every minute asking
her superior to pray for her, yet who herself did
nothing to be freed from the temptation."

It is evident that when one placed herself under

Mother Thérèse it was not sufficient to cry: "Lord,
Lord"; it was necessary to act, to act simply yet
bravely. For a further example: some religious
showed their happiness because Father Gautrelet
came to give the retreat to the community at
Lyons. "It is true," said Mother Thérèse, "that
among the Fathers some are holier than others. But
I believe they keep it for themselves, that sanctity.
We must understand that if we would acquire a
little of it, it is necessary that we ourselves do the
work, that it may be the fruit of our labor; with,
of course, the aid of divine grace, for without that
we can do nothing; with it, we can do all things."

The questionable enthusiasms of her daughters,
Mother Thérèse ever tested by her great practical
sense. Little did she care to hear them cry out for
suffering—cries that the slightest pain experienced
changed into complaints.

A religious, who in Mother Thérèse's judgment
was too ardent, once cried out in recreation, "Lord,
deprive me of everything, but give me souls." "Yes,
Sister," asked Mother Thérèse, "and what would
you have left to give to souls if God deprived you
of everything?"

Virtue, with Mother Thérèse, was never separated from interior calm and self-possession. She
expressed her ideal in this longing: "Let us pray
that our houses may be in very truth Cenacles
wherein the Spirit of God may come in order to
animate each one and dispose her to fulfill with
perfection the work entrusted to her."

The duties of one's state in life should be fulfilled even unto perfection, with the calm belonging to the Cenacle, in the love and union and expansion of hearts. "For," Mother Thérèse loved to say to young religious, "we should never allow even one thought of sadness to enter the soul. Have we not within us Him Who is the joy of heaven!"

"Believe me when I say that an obedient religious is a happy religious, because she makes of all her actions so many spiritual communions. . . ."

One understands therefore, how souls that would lend themselves to such teaching gave forth joy, much the same as the nightingale coming every morning at time of meditation would sing its measured strains of harmony outside the chapel window.

One day, during community recreation, a sister spoke of the singing of the little bird that came so faithfully every morning. Mother Thérèse heard her and said, "I am afraid that because of the desire to hear that bird, we will no longer hear the good God." The story goes that after that, the nightingale never came again. "I'll wager, Mother," said one of the sisters, somewhat saddened, "that you ordered him to depart." A smile was the only answer Mother Thérèse gave. The great love of God sang its own canticle in the souls of her daughters. When they were with their Mother they were happy.

The expressions of regret made by those who through obedience had to depart from Tournon, are, therefore, not surprising. Such regrets being written quite simply to Mother Thérèse by one of the Mothers, the former answered: "You need have no regret that you were not here during the past winter, because you have where you are as many, and even more, opportunities of advancing in holiness."

That Mother sent far away from Tournon might well have replied to her former Superior: "It is the warmth of your heart that I need in order that I may be filled with the love of God."

Mother de Larochenégly asked Mother Thérèse to rekindle by this warmth of her maternal heart a poor sick soul whom she sent to her.

One day one of those Mothers whom the angel of darkness had deceived during those happenings in Paris, disembarked from the boat at Tournon. Shortly after the Paris events, she had come to her senses and asked to be readmitted into the Cenacle, and the Mother General in consenting to her request felt she could not do better than to place her under the care of Mother Thérèse. The latter tended this bruised reed with such love, aroused this still smoking flax with such delicate hand, poured the oil and wine of the Good Samaritan into these wounds, still open, with such affection and such patience that Mother de Larochenégly was moved to write after a visit to Tournon, "I stand in admiration before the kindness and the goodness of Mother Thérèse."

Again within the fold, this religious, healed by

this wealth of love, bound herself to her benefactress by the bonds of most tender gratitude. Deeply touched by that gratitude, Mother Thérèse wrote to her one day: "My heart remains united to yours; and although I have not often told you of it I hope you have never doubted the fidelity of my heart, as I have never doubted yours."

And then, with infinite delicacy: "Long have our two hearts known each other, and it seems to me they have always understood each other."

Of that understanding Mother Thérèse, moreover, gave the true reason. It was the dark night of those Paris days, the error, the failure. But since to recall that past suffering in those words might cause pain, the sensitive soul of Mother Thérèse knows just what to say without giving offence, and from her heart she writes: "One of the things that has fastened the bonds of our friendship more firmly is suffering. To a wounded soul the most comforting words are, 'I understand you and I love you!'"

And now, alas, we must pass from these happy days to La Louvesc. Mother Payan being superior of the house there, Mother Thérèse again retired into obscurity.

During the winter of 1857-1858 the community at Tournon did not know the attractive joys which it had known through the previous winter. She who was the true Mother was no longer superior, but simply one among others, a daughter of her who ruled. Her work again was the work of giving

good example: she edified, but she could not, as in
the previous year, show forth the goodness of her
heart.

Her life kept its unchanging, peaceful course.
Perhaps the sole event we might mention was the
report which at this time was whispered about
with such consolation. Since February 11th, in a
little village of the Pyrenees, a Lady had appeared
to a peasant girl; a spring of water which would
heal the sick had sprung up!

The miracles witnessed there were often the subject of conversation at community recreations.
Lourdes did not, however, win acceptance at once
from the venerated Mother. We will later learn
how she came to have faith therein. We may well
suppose that her prudence restrained the enthusiasm of the young sisters more than once. Not only
did her hesitation show us how Mother Thérèse
was little inclined to give credence to extraordinary happenings, but the Church had not yet
pronounced on them, and it was the part of wisdom to wait.

Towards the end of August, the community left
Tournon. Mother Thérèse was sent to Montpellier. We must follow her there, for henceforth
God's action upon her is most intimate, most direct.

For the first time, so far as we know, Mother
Thérèse is chosen to be the recipient of extraordinary graces and illuminations.

XIX. The Spouse of the Canticle

THE PATH of humility which God had selected for His servant led her, as is the way with God, to mount to the highest heights of the mystical life. This life, which is often termed extraordinary, began with Mother Thérèse about 1862. Unfortunately in this, as in her previous life, she remained in the shadow. But let us thank God that He permitted, for our edification, that some of her letters should remain to us.

Up to this time, the spirituality of Mother Thérèse was a spirituality of complete self-surrender.

One instance, chosen from a thousand such, will show us how far she carried that self-denial. The story is told that at the Cenacle at Lyons Mother Thérèse very much desired a hand-rail in the tribune for the sick. A certain elderly woman offered to defray the expenses for the erection of the hand-rail. Mother Thérèse went to announce the good news to her Superior, but she suddenly checked herself in front of her door, and said to herself, "What! I am willing to break my silence for that. Surely I can wait until recreation." And then she went to weep before the Blessed Sacrament because something outside of God could still give her such feeling of joy.

As a soul dead to everything, Mother Thérèse

divided her life between labor and prayer, for work, she would say, is a duty from which the attraction of prayer does not dispense us. Moreover, we do not believe that before her coming to Montpellier she had experienced any of the greater delights of prayer. For years Mother Thérèse had prayed, as it were, in the way of duty, lost in the sense of her own nothingness rather than in contemplation of the Divine. Her spiritual life resembled in more ways than one her life of labor when she would spend hours in turning up sods, or weeding the garden paths. But it seems that God had now completed writing the prologue of her life. The humble servant of all, Mother Thérèse had attracted the favor of the Spouse, and the Spouse led her to His own abode. From 1860 to 1885—that is, for a quarter of a century—the humble Mother was raised, we may well believe, to the sublime heights of prayer.

This admirable intercourse—*admirabile commercium,* as the Church terms it—between God and her is what we will now study. We will confine ourselves to such happenings as best serve to frame the marvelous picture which God is about to paint.

Mother Thérèse reached Montpellier on August 30, 1860. There she followed her usual life, assuredly never suspecting the great change which God was about to effect in her. In fact, God, Who willed to purify His chosen tabernacle once more before entering the closed doors of her soul, sent

her one of the most crushing blows that she had
ever received.

In September, 1860, a month after Mother
Thérèse's arrival, she had received a visit at Montpellier from Father Renault. That visit was consoling indeed to her heart. For a long time the
Father and his daughter had conversed with each
other in the Lord. They spoke of the late trial in
Paris as the saints know how to speak of human
failings; and, full of supernatural confidence, they
had parted.

Then suddenly, on December 9th, Mother
Thérèse hears that Father Renault is dead. The
Blessed Virgin had come to seek her servant that
he might complete his celebration of the Feast of
the Immaculate Conception in heaven.

God alone knows the acuteness of the suffering
which Mother Thérèse experienced.

We are able to conjecture something of it when
we read between the lines of that letter which she
at once wrote to Mother de Larochenégly. Below
are some extracts. The letter, as we will see, is a
long song of thanksgiving for all that the Cenacle
owed to Father Renault.

"Montpellier, December 11, 1860.

"MY MOST REVEREND MOTHER:

"Blessed be God! That phrase should ever be on
our lips; as readily when He afflicts as when He

consoles. But what a blow has the good God struck our poor Congregation! By the death of holy Father Renault it has lost not only its most faithful and most devoted friend, but its Father and its Founder. This last title is his by right, for has he not led the Congregation to what it is now? Was it not he who understood the work of Father Terme; was it not he who carried it out?

"Now that he seems to have abandoned it, will he forget it? No: I am certain that we have in him a powerful protector with God. We will pray to him that he choose his own successor, that he make known to us the one who, animated by his zeal and his devotion, will be capable of filling the void which his passing has caused in our Congregation.

"I hope that the Society will not leave the novitiate without help, so that you would be forced to transfer it to some other place.

"But let us not dwell on that thought; it will only add to the grief which already fills our hearts, particularly your grief, Reverend Mother, who understand better than any one else the magnitude of the loss we have suffered. Father Renault was for you a stay, a counselor, a guide; God will give us again what we have lost.

"I have confidence above all else in the prayers of our novices. They also, I doubt not, were able to appreciate the kindnesses, the devotion, the virtues of our worthy Father—of him who was the perfect religious. His memory will speak often and

. . . I saw written in letters of gold
that word "Goodness,"
which I kept repeating for a long time
with indescribable sweetness;
I saw it, I say, written upon
all creatures animate, and inanimate,
rational or otherwise —
all bore this name "Goodness."
I even saw it upon the chair
which served me for prie-dieu.

I understood then that all the good
creatures have, . . .
and all the services and help
we receive from each one of them,
are a benefit we owe to the goodness
of our God,
who has communicated to them
something of his infinite goodness
so that we might find it in
everything and everywhere.

Saint Therese Couderc
Cenacle Foundress

eloquently to all those who were blessed in knowing him in a more intimate way.

"The last time that I had the pleasure of seeing him, he was passing through Montpellier, and he spoke much of the persecutions against the Church. God wished to spare him the grief of witnessing their outcome. I would say he was then preparing himself for martyrdom, so greatly did he apparently suffer. God reserved for him a more gentle death, but not one less meritorious, for his life had been devoted to apostolic labors. I doubt not that there will be a request that his life be written. And we will ask it on our knees if that be necessary."

But now let us consider attentively the coming of the Master. The Cenacle at Montpellier today has not the same house as formerly. It is a great pity, for that little chapel of the first community would have been, with good reason, as much venerated by the daughters of Mother Thérèse as the tribune at Fourvière. Montpellier, Fourvière! They are the two gardens enclosed wherein the Spouse will meet His bride and lead her to hear the voice of His love.

The first divine advance was the bestowal of a light, a light in perfect harmony with the spirituality of Mother Thérèse (unity is the keynote of the whole action of God).

One day Our Lord led her to understand that word which summarizes His whole Eucharistic

Life, the word that He Himself spoke at the moment of the Last Supper, . . . *Quod pro vobis datum* —"which is given for you" (Luke xxii. 19). . . . To deliver up oneself! This indeed, is the life of the Risen Christ. He is delivered up to His Church. The Church does with His Body as she pleases. . . . It may be left within the Tabernacle, or It may be brought out therefrom—It is delivered up.

Previously this total surrender had repeatedly aroused astonishment in Mother Thérèse. But this morning, so striking was the light, that she was to walk forever after—even unto the end of her life— in its gentle clarity. Let us read what she wrote on the subject during one of her retreats:

"Sunday, June 26, 1864.

SELF-SURRENDER

"Our Lord had often made me understand how helpful it is for a soul desirous of perfection to *surrender herself—offer herself up*—without reserve to the guidance of the Holy Spirit. But this morning it had pleased His Divine Goodness to give me a very special view of it.

"I was preparing to begin my meditation, when I heard the pealing of various bells which summoned the Faithful to assist at the Divine Mysteries. At that moment the desire came over me to unite myself to all the Masses that were being said, and to that end I had directed my intention in order to participate in them.

"Thereupon there came to me a general view of the whole Catholic world, and of a multitude of altars whereon at the same moment the Adorable Victim immolated Himself. The Blood of the Lamb without stain was flowing in abundance over every one of these altars, which seemed to me to be surrounded by a light cloud of smoke which ascended towards heaven.

"My soul was seized and penetrated with a feeling of love and of gratitude at sight of this satisfaction which Our Lord offered so abundantly for us.

"But I was also greatly astonished that the whole world was not sanctified by it. I asked how it was when the Sacrifice of the Cross offered only once was sufficient to redeem all souls, that now being renewed so many times it did not avail to sanctify them all.

"This is the response that I thought I heard: 'The Sacrifice is without doubt sufficient by itself; but souls are lacking in correspondence and generosity. That generosity ought to lead us to *surrender ourselves* to God.' But what does it mean to *surrender oneself?* I understand the full extent of the meaning of the word—*self-surrender*—but I cannot explain it. I only know that it is very vast, that it embraces both the present and the future.

"To *surrender oneself* is something more than

to devote oneself, more than to give oneself; it is
even something more than to abandon oneself to
God. To *surrender oneself* is to die to everything
and to oneself; to be no more occupied with self
except to hold oneself turned towards God. *Self-
surrender* is no longer to seek self-satisfaction in
anything, . . . but only God's good pleasure. It is
necessary to add that *self-surrender* is to follow
that complete spirit of detachment which holds to
nothing, neither to persons nor things, neither to
time nor place. It is to be at everyone's disposal,
to accept everything, to submit to everything.

"But one may perhaps believe that that is a very
difficult thing to do. Do not be deceived; there is
nothing so easy to do, nothing so sweet to practise.
The whole thing consists in making a generous
act in the beginning by saying with all sincerity:
'My God, I wish to be entirely Thine, deign to
accept my offering.' But one must be careful to
keep oneself in this attitude of soul and not to retreat from any of the little sacrifices which can
help one to advance in virtue; to remember always that one has *surrendered oneself*. I pray Our
Lord to give an understanding of this word to all
souls eager to please Him, and to inspire them
with a means of sanctification so easy. Oh! if one
could understand in advance that sweetness and
that peace which one tastes when there is no reserve with the Good God. The *surrendered* soul
has found Paradise on earth, for he enjoys here

something of that true peace which is a part of the happiness of the elect."

To him who knows how to read between the lines, it is evident that Mother Thérèse had surrendered herself, and that God had abundantly rewarded her sacrifice. Moreover, other letters still extant permit of no doubt on the subject.

The first visit of the Bridegroom to His spouse had in it something of that sweetness which Saint Margaret Mary experienced at Paray-le-Monial when Our Lord called her to the divine nuptials. The cross was wholly covered with flowers, the points of the thorns concealed under the roses.

That one may have further evidence on this matter we add these words of Mother Thérèse: "When I have received Holy Communion," she says to her superior, "it is impossible for me to leave the chapel. The time devoted to thanksgiving by the community seems to me so short that I must do violence to myself to follow the sisters to the refectory. And although I go there, I take my breakfast without realizing what I am doing, and without being for one moment distracted from the presence of Our Lord. When I return to the chapel and find myself alone, I am then able to give way to the impulses I have been obliged to restrain, and oftentimes my tears flow copiously. There are days when just the very thought of God so moves me that I am no longer mistress of myself. I would then that I might hide myself from all eyes, and the obligation of remaining in choir causes me a suffering and an unspeakable restlessness."

Another time she confided to the same superior: "I have but one need, but one thought—to pray, always to pray. So strong is that need in me, that on Sunday every minute that I spend outside the chapel I feel like a tormented spirit." It will be seen that God had made Himself complete master of her soul. As usually happens in these special states of prayer, everything except self-absorption in God is an impossibility or a suffering. Mother Thérèse humbly confessed it: "Formerly my spiritual reading was an enjoyment and consolation to me; now, I cannot give my mind to it, nor can I get any relief from the powerful attraction that ever calls to me when I am in the presence of the Blessed Sacrament.

"For my meditation I often read on two subjects, intending to meditate on them the next day. But I find it impossible; two thoughts alternately possess me during the entire time of prayer. The first is that of the holiness of God. I can give my thoughts to nothing else—that sanctity which is my God! The sanctity of God, above all human thought. Everything is in that, for me. Then I am lost in a profound self-annihilation and repeat through the hours: 'Jesus, I adore Thee because Thou art Holy, because Thou art Holiness itself.'

"The second thought is that of my helplessness. I know how to say but one sentence: 'Jesus, have mercy on me.' But that sentence is as a mirror in which I see the needs of the whole world. The appeals which are made to us, all our special intentions, are personified for me in the cry: 'Jesus, have pity on me'; and may I never grow weary in repeating this appeal."

Mother Thérèse is elevated to the prayer of complete simplicity. It is possible that she did not even utter the words which she mentions. This profound vision of the Holiness of God and of her own nothingness prevented her, we have been told, from formulating a prayer. All her prayer lost itself in the divine Holiness, and consequently in her own self-abasement.

This vision of the Holiness of God enabled her to see into one of the divine perfections. So the work of grace continued to operate in her soul; from a more general vision, Mother Thérèse was led to a particular vision. Her eyes, it seems, had caught a glimpse of something special, and of this vision she writes in full detail to her Superior General.

"I had, some days since, a vision which consoled me much. It took place during my thanksgiving. Suddenly I saw written in golden letters the word 'Goodness,' a word which I had been repeating to myself for a long time with inexpressible delight. I saw it, I say, written upon every created thing, animate and inanimate, rational and non-rational —all bore the name 'Goodness.' I saw it even on the chair which serves me as a prie-dieu. I under-

stood then that everything of good which creatures
possess, all the service and the help that we receive
from any one of them, is a favor which we owe to
the Goodness Who has communicated to them
something of His own Infinite Goodness, in order
that we might find it in everything and everywhere.

"But what I say is nothing. Would that I could
express to you what in that moment I experienced.
Alas! the divine cannot be described. Only, I am
no longer surprised that the Saints found themselves ravished by the vision of that Goodness of
which so many souls know so little. This impression remained with me for several days, during
which I was unable to take pleasure in anything,
on account of that which I had seen and experienced."

The Goodness of God! Reading those lines one
might be listening to Saint Ignatius explaining
his famous contemplation of divine love. This is
the Goodness which the author of the Exercises
would have us understand, and it was after having
contemplated it that he felt compelled to cry his
suscipe: "I have received all from Thee; to Thee
I would return all."

It is not surprising that the Foundress of the
Cenacle was thus enlightened in a very particular
way by God, concerning one of the leading points
of those Exercises which she gave to her daughters. Did not God will, by giving such a light, to

teach the Religious of the Retreat that they should
see to it that their retreatants go from the Exercises
with an understanding of the Good God?

Everything here below—both trials and joys—
comes from the Father, from the one Father. To
believe in the Goodness of God, come what may—
that is to say, even on our own Calvary! It is to this
rugged and austere faith that the Exercises ought
to lead us.

About five years before the time of this vision
there died a saint, a contemporary of Mother
Thérèse, who himself had received the mission of
preaching to the world the Goodness of God.

"The good God," the Curé of Ars would say,
"the good God—Behold, I stand with Him." And
almost always his morning catechetical instructions
would end with the habitual refrain which his
heart, so full of love, sang! "My little children, we
should love the good God very much; we should
love the good God very much."

Mother Thérèse loved Him very much. And
after the word "Goodness" had been seen by her,
stamped in letters of gold, on every created thing,
she loved Him so much that more than once her
place in chapel was saturated with her tears.

She loved Him just the same in her trials—when
the good God withdrew Himself and led her, as we
shall see, to share in His mortal agony in the
Garden of Olives.

For a moment, however, this way to which God

was calling her affrighted her, so that she asked
herself, so accustomed was she to the way of abnegation alone, whether or not the new way was
safe.

But one day a Father of the Grande Chartreuse
came to Montpellier. He gave a conference to the
community. His conference ended, the sisters were
withdrawing, when, in a whisper he said to Mother
Thérèse: "Stay where you are. I wish to speak
with you." And the Carthusian spoke with her of
God. Captivated by what he said, she opened her
soul to him, and the Father answered her with
these simple words which were light itself: "The
savor of God can come only from God." After that
she went forward without fear upon the highway
of the great love of Goodness.

While Our Lord was thus filling her soul to
overflowing with His choicest graces, a novice, sent
by Mother de Larochenégly, arrived at Montpellier. She was to play a notable part in the history
of the Cenacle. Was Mother Thérèse specially enlightened with regard to her subject? Did she see
in advance her long, fruitful years as Mother General? We may well believe she did, for that day,
occupying the place of the Superior, she bade the
whole community to rejoice.

The humble Mother had greater reason than all
the others to rejoice, for God had reserved for this
novice the supreme honor of understanding
Mother Thérèse and of making her known to her
Congregation as the true Foundress of the Cenacle.

The Very Reverend Mother Marie Aimée
Lautier was the instrument of God in restoring
order and in lifting humility to glory.

XX. The Garden of Gethsemani

IN 1867 the Superior General closed the Cenacle
at Montpellier and sent Mother Thérèse to
Lyons. When she arrived at Fourvière, the house
had just been completed. The front thereof was
large and attractive. Two wings extended from the
rear into the garden; the wings were in turn connected by the chapel; and across the length of the
chapel, at the second story, ran a gallery.

"It filled me with admiration," said Mother
Thérèse. Her admiration was entirely justified,
particularly if she recalled the day when under the
guidance of the little hunchback of the Place Saint-
Côme, she, with Mother Contenet, first saw the
place, with its ill-suited buildings, without sym-
metry or contour.

Fourvière—the last house in which Mother
Thérèse will live! For eighteen years she will
therein work out her sanctification to completion,
and she will in turn sanctify this blessed place.
Therein she will bring down graces upon every
generation of religious who will succeed her in

the Cenacle. And the chief glory of that house will have been that it has seen a great servant of God grow old and die. And, we may also add, that it has seen her suffer. For the golden letters which but lately formed the word "Goodness" have vanished. The time of the divine nuptials has passed. It is the hour of Calvary, with all its horror.

On this hill of Fourvière, the poor Mother, like unto the Blessed Virgin at Golgotha, is to take her place beneath the Cross. *Stabat Mater dolorosa:* "beneath," without other support to cling to when the earth would be shaken than the Cross itself: "beneath," in tears. *Juxta crucem lacrymosa.*

What we are about to record of this period of her life, all readers will not understand. They only will understand to whom, according to the word of the Gospel, it is given to understand. On the other hand, there is no soul that will not feel something of the bitter suffering which filled this soul in its agony.

About 1875 the vision of the Divine Goodness was withdrawn: Mother Thérèse now knew no other vision but that of suffering.

France had lived through a terrible year. The Commune had made martyrs. The hopes of a religious betterment which some had entertained had crumbled. No beginnings had been made as yet in the realization at Montmartre of that request made by the Sacred Heart to Saint Margaret Mary, nor had any start been made of that great movement of pilgrimage to Paray-le-Monial to supplicate the

Heart of Jesus to save Rome and to save France. No reassuring stars had as yet been kindled in the heavens.

The history of the Church shows us that God chooses at a time when wickedness abounds those whom He would have offer themselves in sacrifice.

It pleased Our Lord to set His Eyes on Mother Thérèse and to offer her this fresh vocation.

The following was the occasion:

A Jesuit, Father Maréchal, came to address the community at Fourvière. Ardent and zealous, he expounded the consecration of self, without reserve, to Our Blessed Lord. Mother Thérèse received the light. Her own Superior, whom Mother Thérèse told of the event, recounts it in turn for us:

"I had been superior at Fourvière," writes Mother Bertier, "for about eighteen months. One day Mother Thérèse sought me out, and with hardly a word of introduction, but with her characteristic simplicity and straightforwardness, said to me practically what follows: 'The Church is suffering very much; souls are being lost; Our Lord is forgotten, outraged. We must make reparation to the full extent of our power and assist Him in saving men. I come to tell you that for some time now I have been pursued by the thought of offering myself as a sacrificial victim. This thought fills me with great fear, but at the same time I cannot keep it from me. I spoke about it to Father Gautrelet, and he counseled me to follow the attraction of

grace. I have offered myself to Our Saviour to
suffer all that He may wish.'—I listened to the dear
Mother with much emotion, but I respected her
humility too much to show her the extent of my
feelings. All I said to her was: 'Our Lord has given
you in this a great grace. You have done well in
cooperating with it.' "

This account agrees completely with the one
which Mother Thérèse confided some years later
to Very Reverend Mother Marie Aimée. To the
latter we owe the following details, which she
heard from the very lips of the servant of God:

" 'For many years I had not known what fear
was; I could not understand how one could know
God and not love Him. I saw everywhere His Infinite Goodness and I was filled with His consolations. For me nothing was painful when it was a
question of serving Him.'

"Then she asked all of a sudden: 'Did you know
Father Maréchal?' I signified that I had. 'That
priest was a man of God. He had the soul of an
apostle. He was invited from time to time to give
conferences to the community. On one such occasion he spoke in particular of unreserved consecration to Our Lord. As if he intended to question
each one of us, he said that the Divine Master asked
for souls consecrated to His Will for the fulfilment
of all His purposes; that is to say, immolated, sacrificial victims for His glory and the salvation of
souls. His words pierced me like a sword and trans-

fixed my heart. That day and for several days
following I continued to hear them, and they pro-
duced in me the same impression. I prayed; I
offered myself to God as completely as I could; I
told Him that I did not dare to offer myself as
victim, for victims to be pleasing to Him should
be pure, and I had so greatly offended Him.

" 'Then He made me understand that He
wanted me, that He accepted me as a sacrificial
victim, and I distinctly heard these words: *You
shall be a victim for the holocaust.* There was in
me no revolt; I gave myself up to His Will completely, but I was atremble, abashed. I asked what
those words, *victim for the holocaust,* meant. Our
Lord explained that the ordinary victim was sacrificed and immolated on the altar, and the parts
remaining were given to the priests and used for
other purposes; but that the fire of heaven descend-
ing on the holocaustal victim consumed it entirely,
so that even the ashes were given to the wind, and
no trace, no vestige of anything that could still be
used remained, for all was for Him.' And she repeated those words: *'for all was for Him.'* "

And from that time on, all assuredly was for
Him.

The Master first took her body. Not one mem-
ber was spared. Unspeakable sufferings tortured
her poor limbs, above all. Deaf, she could not follow the conversation at recreation, and her life
grew more and more silent. "We have three things

to do in this world," she would say; "to labor, to pray, and to suffer. This third thing is never lacking to us."

The ten or twelve years of life still remaining to her did not know, perhaps, one hour free from suffering. But these physical sufferings were but the prologue. Her mission as a sacrificial victim called for further agonies. A word uttered by Mother Thérèse gives us to understand how with a wholly divine delicacy Our Lord before making her share in this new chalice asked her for her consent. Mother Thérèse adds that when she heard this unexpected offer she felt as if she would swoon away and she trembled with fright, but that without hesitation she surrendered herself.

Self-surrender! One remembers the light of Montpellier when the Sun of Goodness shone with its gracious smile over all her days. That light was bestowed expressly in view of what would happen at Fourvière. So, from afar God prepared His chosen one for the sacrifice.

The hour of sacrifice had sounded.

Let us approach the place of holocaust with respect. The Religious of the Cenacle of Fourvière point to it with emotion, and very often in their hours of trial go to kneel there, to ask of God some little measure at least of the strength and the generosity of their valiant Mother.

As in most of the chapels of the Cenacle, the choir of the religious at Fourvière faces the Epistle side. Above this chapel is a small balcony about sixteen feet long by six feet deep. A balustrade rests upon two short columns of red marble. In the corner to the left, was a prie-dieu with a covering of coarse straw. It was in that corner and on that prie-dieu that Mother Thérèse went through perhaps the greatest experiences of her life.

In very truth after Our Saviour had wounded her body, He willed that her soul be crushed by the share He granted her in all His sufferings in the Garden of Gethsemani. Behold her, then, the lowly victim, on her knees, head bowed, hands joined repeating her Master's appeal for mercy; but her words are those of the little ones and of publicans: "My God, have pity on me!" Sometimes they would observe her lift her head, and the half-opened eyes would search the Host in the ostensorium or the door of the Tabernacle.

Thus did Our Lord Himself in the hours of His Agony seek the Face of His Father.

But the Sacred Host showed no greater consolation to Mother Thérèse than did Heaven to the agonized One in Gethsemani, and Mother Thérèse, lost in sorrowful contemplation, would utter anew her heart-rending cry. That cry was nearly always accompanied by sobbing. As Mother Thérèse was very deaf, and did not hear her own weeping, she never knew that everyone in chapel was witness of her agony.

God permitted it, no doubt, so that her children

would not be deprived of such a strengthening sight, and that they might still better understand the treasure which Fourvière possessed.

For almost ten years that blessed corner knew Mother Thérèse, knew her weeping for hours at a time and repeating continuously through those hours: "Have pity on me!" A great number of saints, both men and women, have received this very precious gift of sharing in the Agony of Our Lord. As a rule, however, that favor was not accorded them except from Thursday night to Friday, in remembrance of Gethsemani. But Mother Thérèse, although she wept more on Thursday evening and Friday, once she had entered Gethsemani never left it. Without an angel to console her, she kept watch in her sorrowing soul, even unto death. Why did she thus suffer? For the same cause that led our Master to endure His Agony—the sins of men. And her continuous cry, "Have pity on me!" was an appeal unto the goodness of God that He would not exact justice. There is no evidence to show that her agony was lightened by any vision of the Master Whose suffering she shared. On the contrary it seems that through her tears she saw nothing except sinners, and the evils endured by the Church and by her country.

At Fourvière some invocations which she wrote during these long hours of agony are preserved with great veneration. She wrote them in pencil, with trembling hand, upon the back of an announcement card. That prayer was without doubt written in that chapel by Mother Thérèse as she knelt upon her prie-dieu and was an outgrowth of her accustomed grief. That announcement card bears the date July 21, 1880. One may rightly believe, then, that the prayer written by Mother Thérèse concerned the first great persecution of the religious, brought on by the Government's decrees. We give below the prayer as it was written by the servant of God, and as it is preserved today in the room in which she died:

"How long, O Lord, wilt Thou be *angry with us?*
  My God, have pity on Thy people.
  My God, convert Thy people.
  My God, forgive Thy people.
  My God, look with compassion on Thy people.
  My God, save Thy people.
  My God, come to the aid of Thy people.
  My God, abandon not Thy people.
  My God, show forth Thy power and Thy goodness in favor of Thy people.
  My God, fight for Thy people.
  My God, be moved by the evils suffered by Thy people.
  My God, come and hear the prayer of Thy people who have placed in Thee their every confidence."

It was not long, as one may well suppose, before the little tribune of the Cenacle of Fourvière became the subject of conversation among the Mothers and Sisters.

But they always spoke of it in secrecy, with respect and discretion, so that someone who came to pray for the first time in the chapel, hearing the sighs coming down from the gallery, hastened, affrighted, to inform the Superior that there was someone in the church a prey to great sorrow.

"We can do nothing," answered the Superior (Reverend Mother de Gaudin). "It is Mother Thérèse who suffers and weeps with Our Saviour. You are a newcomer here, but you will hear that often, very often. Mother Thérèse weeps in the tribune. She is so deaf that she believes she cries noiselessly. We suffer with her."

On another occasion—it was on Easter Sunday —one of the Mothers seated herself at the organ to play the accompaniment for Benediction. All of a sudden she heard the sighs. Overcome with emotion, she fled the gallery. To a Mother who would have held her back, she said: "No, I cannot play the accompaniment when Mother Thérèse sobs thus at my side. It upsets me completely." "Have no fear," said Mother de Bridieu to her, "no one has given pain to Mother Thérèse: it is Our Lord who wishes her to feel in a most acute way, more acute on certain days, the offences of sinners."

These simple recitals show us with what reserve the Religious of the Cenacle spoke of their Mother, since all did not know the secret of the mystery.

The mystery of her suffering is also attested by the Mother General, who wrote as follows after the death of the Foundress:

PART THREE: *The Shadow*

"On more than one occasion I have had opportunity to witness this meritorious and sorrowful state in which the most holy Will of God held our venerated Mother. Often have I heard her weep, and even sob, particularly on the evening of Thursday and all through the day of Friday. Because of it I felt an interior quiet that forbade me to speak to her or to seek to console her, as I would have been led to do if it were a question of simply earthly suffering."

The testimony of so high an authority permits no one to doubt the truth of that which many were quietly repeating: Mother Thérèse, having suffered much from the hands of men, suffered a long time from the Hands of God.

If every tear shed here below washed away some offence, who will count the number of the offences washed away by the tears of Mother Thérèse?

If the cross marked over the doorways of the Hebrews hindered the Angel of Justice from entering, who can tell us the number of trials from which others have been saved by Mother Thérèse?

The little tribune at Fourvière will ever remain holy ground. That mysterious corner wherein for ten years a great friend of God wept, will long be an object of veneration.

The Sunset

PART FOUR

The Survey

XX. The Invalid's Armchair

WONDERFUL SUNSETS may often be seen from the end of the garden of the Cenacle at Fourvière. Oftentimes at Lyons, too, in the evening, the heavens, until then hidden by mists, are brilliantly lighted up and look veritably like a picture of fairyland. What panoramas one may enjoy in that secluded garden!

Below is the meeting place of the Rhône and the Saône; on the left is the great city; and in the distance, when the sky is clear, the towering Alps; then, on the right are the hills of Sainte-Foy, behind which the sun sinks to rest. So soft is the misty atmosphere, so limpid the shadings, so harmonious the blend of colors, that one instinctively recalls the great Corot, a contemporary of Mother Thérèse, he who so admirably fulfilled his mission of reproducing the beauty of those appealing pictures which God in His goodness has painted here below for the satisfaction of our eyes.

Towards the evening of the life of Mother Thérèse, a life which the mist had almost continuously hidden, the heavens suddenly lighted up, and an infinite tenderness accompanied the setting of the sun. The clouds were no more; or, rather, what clouds there were, were brightened with a marvelous light. This Mother, unknown, ignored, one who had been looked upon as of the past—indeed they commonly called her "the old woman" —thanks to the new Superior General, suddenly appeared in her true light as the only and true Foundress of the Cenacle.

That Cenacle had been rendered so fruitful by her prayers and her tears that its houses already numbered twelve. They were situated in France and in Italy. Soon the Cenacle will cross the channel and establish itself in England; some few years after, it will be in the United States; then in Belgium, in Switzerland, in Holland. In all of these houses, filled with fervent religious, wholly devoted to the Spiritual Exercises of Saint Ignatius, to works for the little ones, for the lowly, for laboring and professional women, the name of Mother Thérèse is repeated with a respect with which veneration and love are ever mingled. Everywhere the Reverend Mother General journeyed, she told what she knew, and she knew such great, such beautiful truths of Mother Thérèse that all the houses were envious of the favored Cenacle of Fourvière.

From out the shadows came manifold traits which these shadows had hidden, manifold words which one repeated to another, so that little by little about the head of the worthy Mother was set an aureole of light. The sun, which had every day quietly disappeared, was now to set in tender glory, the glory of hidden sanctity.

We will give here some of these sayings of Mother Thérèse, sayings that are unlike any others, filled as they are with something indescribable, something which she drew from those long, sorrowful conversations.

But first of all let us fix before our eyes the background against which most of these words were uttered. The infirmarian of the Cenacle would roll the large straw armchair to the window. At the base of this chair was a board to support the feet of the invalid, which were swollen from illness. Therein, her eyes ever fixed upon her work, the venerated Mother labored. At her side was a little cloth bag, filled with small pieces of paper which were carefully folded. There were twenty-nine of them, each one bearing an invocation from the Litany of the Holy Name of Jesus. From time to time she would stop her sewing; then with a hand almost deformed by rheumatism, she drew one of these little folded pieces of paper, read the invocation, and silently meditated thereon while she resumed the mending of her sisters' clothing.

And now let us listen to some of these words which, while seated in her armchair, she let come forth from her heart: "I am not tired of this world. I wish to remain here as long as it pleases the good God. Since Our Lord has been sentenced to remain here even unto the end of the world, should we not be content to remain here with Him?"

At another time: "My prayer is very simple. I place myself in the presence of Our Lord and I tell Him all that is in my heart. I rejoice with Him in His divine attributes; I long for all creatures to adore Him and love Him. . . . I ask for the perseverance and the sanctification of the just, for the conversion of sinners—in a word, I open my soul before the Divine Majesty. If I know joy, I tell Him of it; if pain, I confide it to Him. I rest, selfless, in His Presence."

And she added a phrase which is like an explanation of her famous "Have pity on me!" of the tribune. "I have an ejaculatory prayer which I love very much. I say it all the day long: 'Jesus, have pity on me!' I find everything in that invocation. Through it, I ask pardon for my sins and I beg the graces which are necessary for me."

The Reverend Mother Superior always took care to assign some religious to be near Mother Thérèse during the mid-day meal.

Generally, one of them has recorded, we had only to sit, doing our work, in the corridor near her room. Once when I was thus on guard I was fortunate enough to be called by her. I entered her room. "You have the same name—Thérèse—as I have," the kind invalid said to me. "You look to me to be very young, and I wish to help you to serve Our Lord. Take my word for it, the first grace to ask for, the grace concerning which we cannot think too often, is the grace of perseverance in our vocation." Then with a smile she added: "I am very old: nevertheless I pray for that grace every day."

On the following day, she summoned me again, and said: "My dear Sister, a grace for which many neglect to ask, yet which is the foundation of all the religious virtues, is a deep faith, an ever-deepening faith. Pray all your life that you may have a deep faith."

One day she said to me in a tone I shall never forget, that one should reflect and pray a long while before asking the good God for suffering, because that was a prayer which God quickly granted. And then . . . The look on her face finished the sentence. I went out, saying to myself: "Our Mother knows whereof she speaks."

Having learned that one of her nephews had decided to come to Lyons to live, she plainly showed her dissatisfaction: "We always tilled the fields; why does this younger generation wish to change the conditions in which God has placed them and come to lose themselves in large cities?"

To one who complained to Mother Thérèse because she had been made the subject of criticism, the venerated Mother said: "Sister, let us strive to fulfill our duty both to God and to our neighbor. When we have done that, let others speak and act as they please. If God is for us, and our conscience does not reproach us, little need we trouble ourselves concerning the judgments of men. For the rest, look upon the Tabernacle. He Who dwells therein understands all, sees through all, and loves us."

On August 2nd, the Feast of the Portiuncula, seeing some religious hastening to gain a great number of indulgences, she said: "As for me, I am more occupied in considering dispositions than quantity."

"Sister," she said once, with her great common sense, to a postulant who had barely tasted the food on her plate: "You must eat; because if you do not, you will not be able to serve Our Saviour generously. Eat, then, or go back to your mountains."

Every one of those who came to sit beside that famous armchair heard some words, so to speak, from God. She had these words for children: "Our souls ought to lie at the feet of Our Lord even as the humble flowers at the foot of the mountains. Then would they receive dew from heaven."

For souls enduring trials, she had these words: "Would that I might comfort you; but I see no other way than for you to abandon yourself to the Hands of Providence. To desire nothing is the most perfect way. . . . Great trials make great souls and fit them for the great things which God wishes to do through them."

To Superiors agonized by the civil laws which threatened the Congregations, she said: "They can, indeed, worry us by vexatious external measures, but they cannot prevent us from loving the good

God and from being wholly His. For those who
see everything in the light of faith, persecutors are
more to be pitied than the persecuted. Let us pray
for them. They are the rods with which God
chooses to chastise us. For this may He be praised.
Events will make known His Will. We should
love that Will at all times."

To souls discouraged, she would say: "Have
confidence in God. The tree of the Cross bears
fruit in every season and in every land. To it I go
always for the mercy of the good God; I always
come away in peace. Let us say bravely and confidently: 'God is sufficient for me.'"

With due respect, she said to a priest: "I asked
the Beloved Apostle to obtain for you the fulness
of the priestly spirit, which he himself drew from
the heart of the good Master, and which makes
priests holy apostles, strong in word and in work."

And above all else there was the word, unheard
by men, the word that brought down the favors
of God, the word because of which all her trials
had been granted her, the word that was even more
close to her than her favorite ejaculatory prayer:
"Have pity on me!" Her lips never uttered it; but
that venerated armchair was witness to it thousands and thousands of times. That word was her
will to live wholly for the love of God, so to live
even unto the end—hidden, unknown, consumed!

* * *

We must record something even better than

words uttered by Mother Thérèse. Her life, apparently so ordinary, was marked beyond doubt by the marvelous. The news that Mother Thérèse performed miracles spread from house to house.

Let us look at some of the extraordinary facts that go to form a glorious aureole about the head of this humble victim.

Mother Thérèse, as we said above, experienced some difficulty in believing in the apparitions at Lourdes and at La Salette. This doubt caused her much pain, and she wished she could free herself of it. In the infirmary at Fourvière there had been for some years a religious who was paralyzed. Mother Thérèse, who always loved the sick, was particularly devoted to this religious. She constantly pleaded with God to make her well. The idea now came to her to ask of the Blessed Virgin the restoration to health of this religious as a sign and proof of the authenticity of the apparitions at Lourdes and at La Salette. To this end she made a novena. On September 8th, the day the novena ended, the religious stood up, cured, and returned to her work in the life of the community.

It is said that from that day Mother Thérèse never again doubted that the Blessed Virgin had appeared on the banks of the Gave and on the hills of Dauphiné. And from that time, also, happy witnesses of the miracle believed more and more in the sanctity of the venerated Mother.

* * *

A little girl of six or seven years, who had been led to a pilgrim shrine, drank the water of a fountain there said to have miraculous power. The child was an orphan. As she was filling her glass, there appeared to her a religious in black habit, with violet cape and white coif. "What are you doing?" she asked the child. "I am drinking this water," the little one answered, "that I may become holy." Then looking upon her in a most kindly way, the religious said: "Yes, may you be good, good, very good."

This occurred in 1883. Some years later, that young orphan entered the Cenacle. When she arrived at the novitiate at Versailles, she came upon a portrait of Mother Thérèse, of whom no one had ever spoken to her. She stood there dumbfounded, for this Mother Thérèse was beyond doubt the unknown one whom she had seen at the fountain.

This was but two years before the servant of God left this earth for heaven. At that time Mother Thérèse was pinned down to her armchair; at best, she could walk, with the aid of her cane, only from her cell to the tribune in the choir.

* * *

And this last fact. The door of Mother Thérèse's room opened one day and admitted a religious who for very special reasons desired to converse with her. The reason will appear as we go on. What follows is borrowed from Father Longhaye:

"The year was 1880. The place, the novitiate at Versailles. Certain nights, according to custom, the sisters of the Cenacle kept watch, in turn, before the Most Blessed Sacrament. One night, a young sister who had taken her first vows, and who was beset by interior troubles of soul, was waiting in a room adjoining the chapel for the moment when she would take her place at the watch.

"Through a glass door she saw a light approaching, which she took to be that of Mother Boullier, coming to seek her. She was about to start forward in order to follow her, but remained there dumbfounded on seeing enter the room, the door remaining closed all the while, not Mother Boullier, but some venerable person, unknown to her. The inexpressibly humble and blessed countenance radiated the light which illumined her head, then her whole body, and shone clearly all about her. This young religious had never seen Mother Thérèse, and yet her first thought was: "This is she." Her heart beat as though it would burst, but she had no fear. As the light increased, Mother Thérèse drew nearer, but not by walking. Her gaze penetrated the soul of her daughter to its depths, and the torments gave place to a deep peace. That daughter no longer doubted that Our Lord would give her the grace always to conquer temptation and to serve Him faithfully even unto death.

"No words were exchanged. The young sister, like Saint Peter on Thabor, would have been glad to prolong her happiness; but the light insensibly diminished. Mother Thérèse was disappearing. In a short while only her features were distinguishable: then she faded from sight, in the same glimmering light that had heralded her coming.

"The sister spent her hour before the Most Holy Sacrament in returning thanks.

"The next day, sweetly refreshed, strengthened, and consoled, although convinced that Mother Thérèse was dead, the young religious timidly asked if any news had come from Lyons. Was Mother Thérèse ill? She consulted with her confessor. He said she was mistaken in thinking that God granted extraordinary manifestations of this kind only to the blessed. He obliged her to tell all she had experienced to her superiors.

"At first her recital was not generally credited. In order to put it to some test, a photograph of the venerable Foundress was casually shown to her who claimed to have had this experience. She recognized it at once, save for the eyes, which meant nothing to her. 'The eyes I saw,' she declared, 'had seen the good God.'

"About the middle of the year 1881, obedience made this same religious one among others who were to make part of a new foundation. It was necessary that she pass through Fourvière and remain there a week." [1]

One can imagine with what emotion this young Mother entered the cell of the venerable Foundress at Fourvière. Some days later she wrote to her superior: "How happy I am! I have found the eyes which have seen the good God!"

We may add that, Mother Thérèse having learned, through some indiscreet conversation, something of this extraordinary happening, at once begged the Mother General to put an end to the talk.

The Mother General had great consideration for the humility of the Foundress, but she could not prevent the gradually disappearing sun from sending its bright rays through the heavens.

XXII. The Last Ray

IT WAS of an infinite beauty. God truly seemed to wish to reward the long obscurity of this life which had spent itself in the practice of humility.

Let us enter the cell of this Mother with all reverence. Let us kneel down and behold how captivating is the picture God unfolds to our eyes.

The Reverend Mother General testifies to the facts which it remains for us to tell.

"On January 9th, 1885," she writes, "I left Paris to witness, as I thought, the last breath of our venerable Mother. She had had a sinking spell, and for many hours now had been unconscious. On

arriving at Fourvière, Saturday, January 10th, I
found her in a state of extreme weakness; her face
had become emaciated, her hands were burning
hot. But her expression was calm and altogether
serene, she was entirely conscious, and her mind
was clear.

" 'Strength has gone from me,' she said to me.
'Let it be as the good God wishes. I suffer much, I
am all suffering. Why did you come? You will not
last if you endeavor to attend all your daughters
who are ill.'

"The next day Mother Thérèse expressed the
wish to see me and to be alone with me."

And now we must piously listen to the all-im-
portant communication she then made to her Superior. So strangely beautiful are the facts she
revealed, that we have termed them the sun's last
ray. She told these wondrous truths with her customary humility; but who would not be deeply
moved, listening to the record of the marvels that
occurred during the last months of her life, in the
little cell where she had so often shared in the
Agony of Our Lord!

" 'I do not know what is happening,' she said to
me, 'but since Our Lord has permitted that I may
speak to you, I will speak as I would speak to no
one else. One might think that illness has robbed
me of my right senses. Since yesterday, I have been
surrounded by a multitude who unceasingly pray
and pray, in penetrating tones, and a reverence beyond anything I have ever known. They chant also

hymns, psalms, and liturgical prayers, in solemn
tone. They supplicate, they moan with pain, they
adore the Divine Majesty. They praise that Majesty with a unity, a harmony, a faith, a hope, a
love ineffable. I believe they are the souls in Purgatory. For hours at a time I am thus taken up in
them, for in spite of myself I am forced to join
them. At times I am affrighted, for they envelop
me, they draw very close to me. They are suffering
and they show it in a heart-rending way. I would,
indeed, be delivered from this; I have asked Our
Lord to deliver me, but He does not hear me.'

"When Mother Thérèse had told me this, I
counseled her to tell all to her confessor. She
obeyed. When I visited her again, all smiles, she
looked at me and said: 'The Father told me not to
fear. He believes that these are the souls in Purgatory. Since they are friends of God, because they
love Him and are beloved by Him, they are in His
Eyes a blessed society. I have not slept this night.
They have not left me. I have seen among them
some of our own. I have seen many priests and religious. After I had received the Sacred Host this
morning, they intoned the *Te Deum*. At the
fourth verse, in spite of every effort I made to be
attentive as usual to Our Lord, I was forced to follow them and to sing with them: *Holy, Holy, Holy,
Lord God of Sabaoth.*

" 'It was most wonderful. I would have to live a
very long time before I could forget that harmony,
those accents, that reverence of which nothing on

earth can give even a suggestion. Every verse was sung with a feeling suited to the praise or the appeal which it expressed. When they came to the last verse—*In thee, O Lord, have I hoped: let me never be confounded*—they sang it at least ten times, with a humility, an ardor, a confidence overflowing with love. They are there all the time. I cannot understand why they are not heard. Don't you hear them now?'

"Again she said to me: 'They are a multitude. Among them are the voices of men, the voices of women, the voices of children. . . . Oh, how they pray: how they sing! Oh, if we could pray as they do! How rough, how unbecoming, in comparison is our way of praying! Where, indeed, is our reverence?' "

Such is the recital of the Mother General. Sweet, indeed, is that ray of light which she makes known to us as it bathed the countenance of that great and humble soul. Apparitions of the souls in Purgatory are not rare in the lives of the Saints, but never perhaps until now did those friends of God appear in such radiant light. To hear those multitudes sing the *Te Deum,* to hear them tell of their joy that they will not be confounded forever, brings inexpressible peace to the heart. Death seems less bitter when there is every reason for hoping that it will be followed by these *Te Deums,* full of love, these shouts of triumph unto the holiness of God: "Holy, Holy, Holy, Lord God of Sabaoth." Such is the lesson of supreme confidence that we learn at

[189]

the foot of this bed of agony, in the light of the last ray.

Mother Thérèse taught us this lesson, as she taught us so many others, without even suspecting that she was giving it. These lessons are the lessons of the truly humble.

Towards the end of August, it was certain that the sun was about to set. The Mother General, summoned once more, came again: but when the patient was said to be somewhat improved, she went away. She was never again to see Mother Thérèse alive.

Then the venerable Mother, like unto all who are humble, withdrew into silence. The gates were closed. For one moment, however, she came forth from that deep retirement to utter a word which God assuredly inspired her to utter. That word expressed the supreme will of the Foundress, the last testament of her heart to her daughters.

One of the Mothers who watched by the invalid had the happy thought of asking her which of all the virtues the Cenacle ought especially to cultivate.

At this unexpected question, Mother Thérèse gave a start. Her poor eyes opened, those eyes which, as the young religious of the night adoration said, had seen the good God, and from her lips, now all but lifeless, fell these words:

"I beg God that we do nothing for show, but that we do good in a hidden way, looking upon ourselves always as the most lowly in the Church of God."

She who was about to die had ever regarded herself as the most lowly. Because of that, she had always been kept in a corner—a corner in all the communities in which she had lived, and for ten years in the corner of that tribune at Fourvière. Because of that, she had without complaint accepted all, even that suffering which had become the habitual state of her soul.

And because of that, she accepted the complete abandonment of God at the last hour; for on September 2nd she had said, with tears, that she feared she lacked patience, and a Mother who was present had read from a book a passage, the theme of which was that the friends of Our Lord must endure more than others, and Mother Thérèse had added: "And without consolation!"—words which made such an impression that all the religious at her bedside had the same thought, which they expressed in the same way: "How much God has asked of her!"

And now, the lowliest one of God's Church goes forth without noise, without pomp, surrounded by a few Mothers and a few Sisters who, save for perhaps the last five or six years, knew not what she truly was.

The Superior at Lyons, Mother de Gaudin, has left us the story of Mother Thérèse's last days. She wrote it a few hours after the venerable Mother's

death and addressed it to the Very Reverend
Mother General:

"MY VERY REVEREND MOTHER:

"Our holy victim ended her suffering today,
Saturday, at a quarter past four in the afternoon.
The Blessed Virgin wished that she should go to
heaven on the day consecrated to her.

"The preceding night had been a wretched one.
This morning Our Lord came again and consoled
and strengthened His faithful servant. But her
altered face, her hard breathing, warned us that
the hour of her deliverance was not far off. Her
painful cries never ceased. It was heartrending to
hear them. Almost the entire morning we had
prayed at her bedside. The dear sufferer had been
unable since yesterday to utter a word. But when
we spoke very loud, she could hear us, for her
mind was perfectly clear.

"After reciting Vespers, I returned to her bedside with Reverend Mother de Montaigu. Her
last agony had begun. We recited the prayers for
a departing soul. I blessed her in your stead and I
recommended to her your intentions and those of
the entire community. Her eyes answered me.

"I sent for Father Monnot, that he might come
and give her the last absolution and the plenary
indulgence. She seemed to wish to receive them
again. A few moments later Father de Damas bestowed on her again the absolution and the in-

dulgence. When he had left, we recited the Rosary, the Litanies of the Blessed Virgin and of the Holy Name of Jesus. We invoked Our Lady of the Cenacle, Saint Regis, Saint Victoire, and Father Terme. We had placed on her bed all her holy statues, her book of rules, the cross of her vows, her rosary, her crucifix, which I presented to her to kiss, from time to time, while I repeated the formula of the vows. At the moment her agony began, the cries ceased; one heard nothing but the difficult breathing.

"Just before her last breath, Mother Thérèse opened her eyes, over which there had not fallen the veil that is the usual precursor of death. Gently she fixed her gaze on something that attracted her attention at the foot of the bed; it was there that for some days past we had placed an image of Our Lady of Deliverance. A holy reverence held us, for we felt Our Lady of the Cenacle was there to help her well-beloved daughter. I cannot describe for you, Very Reverend Mother, what passed in my heart at that moment. One felt an influence wholly supernatural. Then the eyes of our holy Mother were lowered again, and they resumed their habitual expression of profound recollection. They would open again to contemplate forever the splendors of eternity.

"It was a quarter past four when our Mother peacefully breathed her last breath and I received her last tear. . . .

"We said the *De Profundis,* and twice recited

the *Magnificat*. It seemed to me that in the measure that this soul would see Our Lord face to face, she would ask us to thank Him for so many graces and so much suffering.

"We are soon going to lay out the saintly remains. I will do it for you, Very Reverend Mother, with veneration and with love,—and for myself, whom the Lord, despite my unworthiness, has chosen to give back into His Hands the Foundress of our dear family. How completely one should correspond to such a grace!

"We have a saint in heaven! What joy for the Cenacle on high to greet this holy Mother!"

On September 29th, the feast of Saint Michael, the body of Mother Thérèse was taken to La Louvesc. "Fifty-seven years before," writes Father Longhaye, "she as a young superior came to take charge of this House of Saint Regis. Its ultimate work was then a mystery both to her and to the Founder himself. She re-entered it after death, accompanied in spirit by her religious family, who only for the previous few years had restored to her the titles of Mother and of Foundress.

"Already the first snows of winter rested upon the mountains. Nevertheless, mosses were gathered, flowers found, to honor the beloved dead. From six o'clock in the evening the great bell of the church sounded. First in the funeral procession, the cross at its head, was Father Cornuet, with the choir children. The cortège itself was led by Abbé Léon Couderc, vicar to his saintly uncle, Curé of

Saint Martin of Ardèche. It was eight o'clock when they arrived at the house, before which stood the entire village, silent and thoughtful. After the services at Fourvière, La Louvesc witnessed her public funeral. Then a last farewell was said to the remains of her whom all regarded as their treasure.

"On the thirtieth, a funeral Mass was offered. Before the Holy Sacrifice began, Father Carry addressed to the congregation words full of sympathy and hope:

" 'My Brethren:

" 'Before this coffin which encloses the body of the venerated Mother Thérèse Couderc, my thoughts, my feelings are even as your own. We are here to fulfill the obligation of gratitude, to unite our sorrow with the sorrow of this house. We are here to join our feelings, our regrets, our prayers to the feelings, the regrets and the prayers of this religious family of which Mother Thérèse was the Foundress and the Mother. Her beautiful and pure life is well known to us. She belongs to us. She is one of the glories of this our mountain. Here she lived. Here she prayed. Here she did good and consecrated herself. Here her heart has rested. To us she gave her fuller, her more generous years. Her name from henceforth is one with the history of La Louvesc. This place cradled her labors. It remains the center from which her labors radiate afar.

" 'It was her wish that she rest here in death.

Her body will sleep here in the silence of the coffin, beside the glorious tomb of Saint Francis Regis. May this coffin some day be opened by the power of sainthood, in the glory of a miracle!

"'May Heaven join in a common glory the tomb of the daughter and the tomb of the Father! Amen!'

"While the absolution was being given, the great bell sounded again. The Coadjutor Sisters, by virtue of traditional privilege, accompanied the coffin to the grave, to which it was borne by her countrymen, followed by the entire population of the town.

"The Choir Sisters went out into the garden and from there followed with their eyes the burial procession. The snow had ceased to fall. The sun had risen in its splendor. Heaven and earth seemed to make festival for the servant of God." [1]

* * *

Both continued to smile because of her. The hope expressed by the Jesuit who preached at her funeral Mass was not slow of fulfillment. Many favors, conversions, healings were granted, and in different countries. Rome will give her judgment on all these. In awaiting her judgment, those whom the Reverend Mother has assisted or is now assisting—for the number of such favors increases every day—keep for her a little of that gratitude which they are showing everywhere to the little Thérèse, the great sower of roses.

Part Four: *The Sunset*

We may remark that the favors granted by Mother Thérèse are particularly directed towards children. Numerous are the healings secured on the last day of the novena, by these little ones. This great and humble soul retains her preferences even in heaven. From the heights of glory she loves with a special love those whom she sought to imitate. It is as if in healing them she but sought to pay her debt of gratitude for the blessedness those gracious models won for her.

EPILOGUE

WE HAVE here and there in this biography compared Mother Thérèse's hidden life with the Eucharistic Life of Our Lord. Before closing our story, we would like for a last time to look upon Mother Thérèse kneeling before the Tabernacle and to sense the deep likeness which exists between her and the small Host.

There are in every life what we may call the interior disposition and the external conduct. The interior disposition is the atmosphere in which the life is developed: the external conduct is, of course, one's actions.

From the moment that He willed to become Man, Christ had descended, choosing thus to abase Himself. He descended from heaven into the womb of the Virgin Mary. He descended from her virginal womb into the manger. After living thirty-three years upon earth, He descended into the tomb. From the tomb, He descended into limbo. After rising again to heaven, He continues to descend—to the altar. Not even here is the sublime descent halted; from the altar he descends still lower—into our poor hearts.

[199]

A Great and Humble Soul

"Thy lowliness all words transcend
When to my heart Thou dost descend."

But even as He thus empties Himself He pours forth goodness.

Goodness, really, is the unfolding of power. One is not termed good unless he possess power in some way. Power like that of the paternal authority that a father possesses; or intellectual power, such as a learned man has; or the power of material possessions, as in the case of the rich.

Goodness, therefore, accompanies authority. To speak more accurately, the true exercise of authority is goodness. One might be ever ready to render service, to place himself at the disposal of others. That would be generous, one would show the spirit of self-sacrifice; that would not yet be goodness.

One might weep with those who weep. That would be kindness, compassion; it is not yet goodness.

What then is this goodness?

Three special characteristics give that sweep of the wing to goodness which lifts it above devotion and kindness and compassion:

It gives always.

It gives without distinction.

It gives without asking any return.

Do you seek a comparison? Then let us take the source of a river.

Epilogue

When did it spring up, this source? The trees which shade it were not as yet planted when the little source itself flowed on.

Days followed days, nights succeeded nights, months, years, centuries passed, and all that time the spring flowed on, apparently useless—for long known, perhaps, only by the clouds and the birds.

But it flowed on, it flowed so well, so regularly, that it formed a stream, and the stream became a river, and the river developed into a torrent of water which ran to the sea.

All this while the source itself, hidden under the moss, is content simply to flow, to flow for all without distinction. Does the source make choice among those who come to it to taste its refreshing water?

Finally, the source gives without looking for any thanks. Indeed, as soon as it has given of its water, its buries itself underground, as if to avoid our thanks.

* * *

Thus is it with the Goodness of Christ in the Holy Eucharist.

Two thousand years ago a word opened up this Source Divine. Since then, It has continued to flow, never ceasing to pour forth Its saving flood. No matter whether one comes to draw therefrom or not, It flows on.

And It also flows for all without distinction.

The door of the house of God is wide open. At the holy table the priest gives to each one the same Bread.

And, finally, It flows without looking for thanks. For the few grateful souls, how many indifferent ones there are!

* * *

We do not think we are guilty of excess when we compare the disposition and the action of Mother Thérèse with the disposition and action of Our Lord in the Holy Eucharist. Her constant gaze upon the Tabernacle, her attentive looking upon the consecrated Bread, had, as it were, assimilated Mother Thérèse to this Sacrament of Love.

From the day when, in her thirty-third year she descended from the office of Superior General, she had made her own the state of self-annihilation. Lowered, first to second place, and very soon to the last, she accepted the place given her, like in this to Our Lord, Who never chooses the spot where the priest will place the ciborium.

Whether she were in a hidden corner of the community, imposing silence upon herself, or in the tribune, where she found her consolations in tears, or in the window-seat of her poor cell, doing the mending—for all those years Mother Thérèse was not even noticed.

It seems, then, that the duty of her state of life, as that of Jesus in the consecrated Host, was to

Epilogue

empty herself. That duty, painful as it can be, she accepted; better still, she loved it.

Yet this venerable Mother, a silent and hidden victim, will be also an active force, a power of goodness. Mother Thérèse was ever the lowly source which flowed, flowed for all, and flowed without looking for thanks.

Have we not seen that she was a source of goodness to her Mothers and her Sisters, without distinction? No feeling of spite ever touched her soul. It was not only on the objects seen in her ecstasy at Montpellier that letters of gold were written. They were engraven also on every intention, every word, every action of Mother Thérèse. As to gratitude, she did not concern herself with it. She saw, without complaining, several generations of religious pass before her who did not even seem to know that she had founded the Cenacle. A day came, however, when they would have liked to thank the source; the source had retired underground.

This lesson of the emptying of oneself, of active goodness, remains the supreme lesson of Mother Thérèse to her daughters.

It can never be learned too well. To give the Exercises properly, to "pour Jesus Christ into souls," as Father Olivaint said, one must be something of Christ; one must have Christ's attitude and follow the conduct of Christ. The Religious of the Cenacle will learn from their Mother how to become victims.

The lesson is all summed up in what every one of them feels compelled to ask herself as she enters that poor cell at Fourvière, which has been left just as it was when Mother Thérèse died.

To the left, against the wall, is the bed, on which rests the crucifix. At the foot of the bed is the straw armchair; in front of it, the prie-dieu from the tribune. . . . There is also a table, and, in a corner, a glass case under which are reverently kept some things that she commonly used. If one were to take these out of the case and place them on top of the mantlepiece and the table, the room would look just as of old. There is the invalid's walking stick, her spectacles, her thimble, her scissors, the little bag filled with invocations to the Holy Name of Jesus, some statues, one or two little books, and her work basket.

Little souvenirs, these, of the cell of one of the elect, which without doubt the faithful will one day come to venerate, as they now go to the room at Ars to venerate the things that belonged to that Saint who, at about the same time, lived by emptying himself, who bestowed goodness upon all who came to him. He and Mother Thérèse are two of the great humble ones of the nineteenth century.

That is why, even as they crowd now at Ars into the poor room of the holy Curé, they will one day, we hope, also crowd into the little cell of Mother Thérèse, where the souls in Purgatory came to chant with her their joyful *Te Deum*.

APPENDIX A

Humility Lifted to Glory

> The author of this book, Rev. Henry Perroy, S.J., had the privilege of being present at the Beatification of her whose spirit he has unforgettably caught in his title A GREAT AND HUMBLE SOUL. It was at St. Peter's in Rome, on November 4, 1951, by solemn decree of Pope Pius XII of holy memory, that Mother Thérèse became Blessed Thérèse Couderc. Shortly after the magnificent ceremonies of glorification, Father Perroy delivered a panegyric on the new Beata. The following is an extract.

EVERY FOUNDRESS of a congregation must sow the seed from which will come forth a new tree for the glory of God. But she must also, and above all else, build up the members of her congregation for the fulfillment of the purpose for which the Church approves it. Thérèse Couderc sowed that mysterious seed in the hostel of La Louvesc which was converted into a retreat house.

But what of the second role? At first sight it seems she did not accomplish that. How could she have done so in the humble duties assigned to her by Providence? Be not deceived. What are the Religious of the Cenacle supposed to do? Give retreats, and above all—it was Father Terme's formal command—the Exercises of St. Ignatius. In his discourse delivered on the occasion of the public audience of November 5th, 1951 (the day following the beatification of Mother Thérèse Couderc) His Holiness, Pope Pius XII, dwelt at length on the Exercises of St. Ignatius: "that small yet mighty book, which by special vocation the *religious must give in private, but without any alterations.*" To give the Exercises, to help souls whom a priest turns over to her, the religious must live these Exercises herself. Jesus, the Gospels tell us, first practiced what He preached: *"Coepit facere et docere."* The blessed foundress of the Cenacle trained her daughters in giving the Exercises, not by teaching them methods, not by telling them how to explain certain truths, but living them. The lesson she taught was a lesson of deeds: "Live the Exercises; you can always give them well when you live them."

Yes, she lived them—not in ordered sequence, of course, but as she was inspired each moment. But she did live them. She practiced the great offering of courageous souls who, wishing to prove still more their love for Our Lord, are not satisfied with serving Him merely, but yearn to render Him the greater sacrifice of accepting humiliations with joy. This she did by going through a living death for thirty years. She practiced the third degree of humility by *seeking* humiliations out of love for Christ and for the sake of resembling Him still more. She went through the first phase of the Exercises—on sin—by being for almost eighteen years a victim of reparation for sinners. She lived the phase on the Passion: for years she drank from the chalice of Gethsemani. She lived the famous contemplation for obtaining divine love; the contemplation of loving God by seeing in every creature that serves us a reflection of the Goodness of God. Finally, she lived the great climactic prayer, "Take, O Lord, and receive," by surrendering everything to her Master, by dying to everything and to herself, by never seeking herself either in persons or in things.

Ah! I know it well. She did nothing but live the Exercises. Not a word escaped her lips. But her silence was worth as much as all she did not say—all the conferences she never gave—all the lessons she never taught—all the directions she never passed on—all the rules she never wrote. The Gospels tell us that St. Peter was recognized by a servant in the court of Caiphas on account of his Gallilean accent. "You cannot deny it; you are a disciple of this man." "Your speech betrays you." Jesus, however, did not only preach. "Jesus autem tacebat. . . . But Jesus was silent." As one can be recognized to be His disciple by a manner of speaking, almost by an accent, so also can one be recognized as His disciple by one's manner of keeping silence. And Mother Thérèse kept silence. . . . Never could she deny that she was a follower of this Man. Her silence proved it well enough.

A Great and Humble Soul

Ah, that silence of Mother Thérèse! That silence is the treasure of treasures of the Religious of the Cenacle. That silence is the pearl of great price in the treasure-chest Mother Thérèse has bequeathed them. It is that silence which has formed them in the past, and will form them in the future. And who can deny that it is through this formation in silence that so many souls receive from them the words that comfort. Knowing how to keep silence is often the way of knowing how to speak. For that matter, may it not be that it is Mother Thérèse's silence that the Church has beatified? At St. Peter's in the famous "Glory" of Bernini, through the passing centuries all types of sanctity have been portrayed—sanctity through zeal—sanctity through charity—sanctity through poverty—the sanctity of innocence—the sanctity of repentance—the sanctity of blood shed in martyrdom. On the 4th of November, 1951, it seemed the Church sang a new canticle: a canticle of *sanctity through silence*.

And Mother Thérèse was silent. . . . Now I understand it all: I understand the admirable oneness of her life. I understand the design of the Divine Sculptor in regard to this soul. I understand all that happened from the 23rd of October 1838, the day of her demotion, until the 26th of September 1885, the day of her death. God wanted to form a Saint of Silence. You could almost say, the patroness of silence in trials. When He allowed her title of Foundress to be taken away from her, it was because He wished to give us cause to admire her silence "in trials coming in the most humiliating guise possible," as Pius XII said. When He allowed her to be relegated to the lowest place it was because there her silence would be most eloquent and best for her formation. Finally, when He allowed the authority due to her rank to be taken away from her it was in order to confer upon her the authority that comes from the Cross. This cross was borne for sixty years in silence. So true it is that God eclipses our vision only to let His own shine forth radiantly.

In the Cenacle, founded by Mother Thérèse, there must reign the purest supernatural spirit. For the purest supernatural spirit was the essence of her life. The purest supernatural spirit means obscurity and silence, two things according to the heart of God, two things which make one sense God. The purest supernatural spirit means, as Mother Thérèse said, not to seek self in anything. Her life was

surpassingly great because it was surpassingly little,

surpassingly upright because surpassingly bent down,

surpassingly public because surpassingly private,

surpassingly eloquent because surpassingly silent,

surpassingly bright because surpassingly shadowed,

surpassingly strong because surpassingly weak,

surpassingly fruitful for God because surpassingly surrendered to God.

APPENDIX B

CONVENTS OF OUR LADY OF THE RETREAT
IN THE CENACLE

United States, Canada, New Zealand

EASTERN PROVINCE

Armonk Road, Mount Kisco, New York
200 Lake Street, Brighton 35, Massachusetts
George Hill Road, Lancaster, Massachusetts
Lake Ronkonkoma, Long Island, New York
Wadsworth Street, Middletown, Connecticut
693 East Avenue, Rochester 7, New York
River Road, New Brunswick, New Jersey
Manalapan, Florida (P.O. Box 8625, Lantana, Fla.)
318 Lawrence Avenue East, Toronto 12, Ontario
268 West Tamaki Road, Auckland E 2, New Zealand
136 Woburn Road, Lower Hutt, New Zealand

WESTERN PROVINCE

3288 North Lake Drive, Milwaukee 11, Wisconsin
513 Fullerton Parkway, Chicago 14, Illinois
11600 Longwood Drive, Chicago 43, Illinois
900 South Spoede Road, St. Louis 31, Missouri
Batavia Road, Warrenville, Illinois
17314 Wayzata Boulevard, Wayzata, Minnesota
5340 Fair Oaks Boulevard, Carmichael, California
Route 1, Box 97A, Rosharon, Texas
5500 St. Mary Street—Box 621—Metairie, Louisiana
3689 Selkirk Street, Vancouver 9, British Columbia

Appendix B

England

33 West Heath Road, Hampstead, London N. W. 3
28 Alexandra Road S., Manchester 16
7 Lance Lane, Wavertree, Liverpool 15
Grayshott-Hindhead, Surrey

Ireland

Military Road, Killiney, Co. Dublin

France

Paris (2)	Lille	Nice
Bordeaux	Lyons	Paray-le-Monial
La Louvesc	Marseilles	Toulouse
(Birthplace	Montpellier	Tigery
of Congregation)	Mulhouse	Versailles
	Nancy	

Italy

Rome (2) *Generalate House* — 260 Via della Balduina		
Genoa	Naples	Turin
Milan	San Giorgio	Biella-Piazzo

Switzerland   Holland   Belgium

Geneva   Tilbourg   Brussels   Abbaye-Kortenberg

Brazil

Rio de Janeiro   Belo Horizonte   Sao Paolo   Fortaleza

Madagascar

Tananarive   Antsirabe   Ambohipo

For further information you are invited to contact the Cenacle nearest you.

[211]

NOTES

CHAPTER I

1 Acts i. 14.

CHAPTER II

1 *Notes de M. l'Abbé Léon Couderc.*

CHAPTER III

1 *Souvenirs sur les premiers temps de la Société* (La Mère Thérèse).

2 *Notes sur la Congrégation* (La Mère Joséphine Grégoire).

3 *Notes de M. l'Abbé Léon Couderc.*

CHAPTER IV

1 *Notes sur la Congrégation* (La Mère Joséphine Grégoire).

CHAPTER V

1 *Notes sur la Congrégation* (La Mère Joséphine Grégoire).

2 *Notes sur la Congrégation* (La Mère Joséphine Grégoire).

3 *Lettre du Père Terme à la Mère Thérèse.*

4 *Notes sur la Congrégation* (La Mère Joséphine Grégoire).

5 *Souvenirs sur les premiers temps de la Société* (La Mère Thérèse).

CHAPTER VI

1 Up to this page of the book in French, Father Terme had always been referred to as "Monsieur" Terme. But now the

author of the French original states he will call him "Father" Terme because by that title all La Louvesc eventually came to address him. (Translator's note.)

2 *Notes sur la Congrégation* (La Mère Joséphine Grégoire).

3 *Souvenirs sur les premiers temps de la Société* (La Mère Thérèse).

CHAPTER VII

1 *Souvenirs sur les premiers temps de la Société* (La Mère Thérèse).—*Notes sur la Congrégation* (La Mère Joséphine Grégoire).

2 *Notes sur la Congrégation* (La Mère Joséphine Grégoire).

3 *Souvenirs sur les premiers temps de la Société* (La Mère Thérèse).

4 "I ask in the second place, how we are a new community, how we are no longer the daughters of Father Terme?" (Letter of Mother Thérèse to M. Lavalette, Vicar at Viviers.)

CHAPTER VIII

1 *Souvenirs sur les premiers temps de la Société* (La Mère Thérèse).—*Notes sur la Congrégation* (La Mère Joséphine Grégoire).

2 *Notes sur la Congrégation* (La Mère Joséphine Grégoire).

3 *Notes sur la Congrégation* (La Mère Joséphine Grégoire).

4 Sister Thérèse, Sister Sainte-Croix, Sister Stanislaus, Sister Joséphine, Sister Augustine, Sister Regis, Sister Marie C., Sister Virginia, Sister Xavier, Sister Agnes, Marie J., Claire P., Dorothy M., Claire L. The names that have not the title of "Sister" are they who were sent by Mlle. Jaricot. Only one of these, Sister Claire Prost, remained until 1839. The others returned to Mlle. Jaricot about 1832; that is to say, the year when the act was signed.

5 *Notes sur la Congrégation* (La Mère Joséphine Grégoire)—*Annales de la Société*.

6 *Vie du Père Terme*.

7 *Souvenirs sur les premiers temps de la Société* (La Mère Thérèse).

A Great and Humble Soul

CHAPTER IX

1 In 1834 there was but one Province of the Society of Jesus in France. It was called the Province of France. Father Renault, Superior of the house at Avignon, was named Provincial in 1833. It was, then, to the only Provincial of the Jesuits in France that Mother Thérèse addressed herself. He resided at Lyons, as did his predecessor, Father Druilhet. This was because of the disturbed state of Paris. In 1836 Father Roothaan divided the Society into two Provinces—Lyons and Paris. Lyons included the houses at Lyons, La Louvesc, Toulouse, Vals and Dôle. Father Renault, at that time Provincial of the Province of France, was named Provincial of Lyons. He held that office from August 15, 1836, to August 15, 1839. Under his government fall those events which shaped the history of the Cenacle.

2 *Notes sur la Congrégation* (La Mère Joséphine Grégoire).

3 *Annales de la Société.*

4 Eventually, the Divine Office of the Church, or Roman Breviary, became the regular Office of the Religious of the Cenacle. (*Décret du Saint-Siège,*—May 16, 1898.)

5 *Notes sur la Congrégation* (La Mère Joséphine Grégoire).

6 *Souvenirs sur les premiers temps de la Société* (La Mère Thérèse).

7 *Notes sur la Congrégation* (La Mère Joséphine Grégoire).

8 *Notes sur la Congrégation* (La Mère Joséphine Grégoire).— *Journal de la Maison de La Louvesc,* 1836.

9 *Souvenirs sur la fondation de la maison de Lyon* (La Mère de Larochenégly).

CHAPTER X

1 *Notes sur la Congrégation* (La Mère Joséphine Grégoire).

2 *Témoignage d'une contemporaine.*

3 *Souvenirs sur les premiers temps de la Société* (La Mère Thérèse).

4 *Annales de la Société.*

5 *Notes sur la Congrégation* (La Mère Joséphine Grégoire).

6 A publication—never put on sale—gave a very unfavorable presentation of the conduct of Mother Thérèse in this matter of

Notes

the separation. When he was called to give testimony in the process held by the Ordinary, the author confessed that he had been led into error.

CHAPTER XI

1 *Notes sur la Congrégation* (La Mère Joséphine Grégoire).— Ménologe de Mme. Gallet.

2 *Notes sur la Congrégation* (La Mère Joséphine Grégoire).

3 *Annales de la Société.*

CHAPTER XII

1 *Notes sur la Congrégation* (La Mère Joséphine Grégoire).

2 *Annales de la Société.*

3 *Souvenirs sur les premiers temps de la Société* (La Mère Thérèse).

CHAPTER XIII

1 *Témoignage d'une contemporaine.*

2 *Souvenirs sur les premiers temps de la Société* (La Mère Thérèse).

CHAPTER XIV

1 *Annales de la Société.*

2 *Souvenirs sur la fondation de la maison de Lyon* (La Mère de Larochenégly).

CHAPTER XVI

1 *Annales de la Société.*

2 But during these years the Sisters worked very hard in the giving of retreats. During this period the foundation of a great work, still in existence, was made—the Congregation of the Children of Mary of Fourvière, founded by Father Nègre. A record tells us that the older Mothers strongly encouraged Mother de Larochenégly to make this foundation. We may rightly believe, therefore, that Mother Thérèse had part in it.

A Great and Humble Soul

CHAPTER XVII

1 *Annales de la Société.*

2 The rough drafts of the Constitutions made by Father Fouillot are not exactly the Rule followed today by the Cenacle. The Congregation preferred to go back to an original draft made by Father Terme and which really is none other than the Rule of the Society of Jesus.

CHAPTER XVIII

1 *Lettres du temps.*

CHAPTER XXI

1 *Origines et fondateurs.* P. Longhaye, S.J.

CHAPTER XXII

1 *Origines et fondateurs.* P. Longhaye, S.J.